Spirit

Of

Selling

Using Universal Laws for

Sales Success

Rhonda M. Petit

ISBN: 978-1-7376744-0-5

Printed in the United States of America

Contents

The Spirit of Selling

DEDICATION

This book is dedicated to my husband Ernie, who is my true love and infinite source and environment for unconditional love and support. He has always seen me for what he calls, "The Real Rhonda," the soul of a change agent.

ACKNOWLEDGEMENTS

I want to acknowledge with gratitude my silent partner in this mission, Infinite Intelligence, who used me to channel this message for you. May you be inspired to unleash and activate your inner power, potential, and passions and be empowered to serve and transform your world with your unique gifts for the harmonious good of all concerned.

Special thanks go to my editor, Gerry Stanek, CEO of Bituminous Press; to my Cover Designer, Eric Labacz, @ Eric Labacz Design; my marketing team Ayo Gospodinova and Carol Kabaale @ AC Empire; my web designer, Angel @haylecreativeco; Tamara Cribley my interior designer @ The Deliberate Page; my branding photographer, Alyse Liebowitz @ 3 Chicks that Click Photography; my videographer Bill Wilusz @ BigGuy Pictures LLC; Kate Allyson, Book writing Coach @ Kate Allyson Creative; Steve & Dawn Siebold, Author/Speaker Coach @ Siebold Success Network; Peggy McColl @ PeggyMcColl Author programs; Bob Proctor @ Proctor Gallagher Institute; David Conway, Mindset & Sales Coach @ Conway Consulting; Ley-Ann Clarke Frederickson, Robbins Results Coach @ Anthony Robbins Companies; Shirzad Chamine & Bill Carmody @ Positive Intelligence. My sincere gratitude and thanks to all of you for your guidance, direction, services, friendship and support along this journey.

Are You Ready for Transformation?

In all thy getting, get understanding. – Proverbs 4:7

Awareness is everything. The journey of life is about gaining more awareness, continual transformation, and serving others with the intent to leave the place better than you found it. It's about making a difference with your talents and doing your part well.

Everyone is selling something every day, and some of us choose to make a career of it. I absolutely love sales. My sales career started with babysitting when I was twelve. My Mom told me a neighbor was looking for someone to watch her newborn daughter while she went to work.

My father was a policeman and my mother was a nurse. I was the oldest of four kids and responsible or babysitting my younger siblings if Mom and Dad were away working or between shifts. At the time, my parents were involved with Amway, and there were always success magazines around the house, with stories from William Clement Stone, Napoleon Hill, Earl Nightingale, and others. I read them all. Each of these writers talked about the secrets that unlock potential—those secrets lie in the subconscious mind, and we are limited only by the limits we place upon ourselves.

William Clement Stone asserted that a sales career is the highest paying profession in the world. The thoughts left me curious and with a growing desire to learn more. We didn't have much when I was little, and I was certainly motivated for financial gain at an early age. I was the oldest and watched my parents transform negativity, lack, and a scarcity mentality, to an attitude of possibility and abundance in their Amway business. Mom and Dad were setting goals and writing them on mirrors with lipstick; hanging up vision boards, buying nice clothes, upgrading automobiles, and taking us on vacations, for the first time.

Likeminded positive people were in the house with them. They were inviting people to meetings, drawing circles, laughing, and having fun. It was like I had two childhoods. This new one was free enterprise in action, and I knew I wanted to be a part of that. I saw the difference in behavior and believed and accepted the principles the magazines claimed to be true.

I went to the next-door neighbor, knocked on her door, and secured my first sale: a babysitting job, five days a week, and a $40 weekly paycheck for the entire summer. There was a feeling of empowerment that came over me and I wanted more.

From there, I went to work at a supper club and worked my way up from coat check girl, to bus girl, to waitress. Go to work in a restaurant, and you'll learn a lot about service. The hourly rate is very small. More than eighty percent of your income comes from tips. This was in the 1980s, and the economy was booming. I used to rake in over $10,000 a year in tips, and I did it all through high school and into my college years. I worked weddings, Christmas parties, and performed tableside dining of Caesars Salads, Steak Diane, Cherries Jubilee, and Bananas Foster.

In my junior year of college, I was a Chemistry major, and Stauffer Chemical was looking for interns. I secured additional part time work with Stauffer, twenty hours a week. After doing lab work for spring semester, I knew I wanted more interaction with people and would not be happy in the lab long-term. Life has a beautiful way of unfolding into new experiences. That job was a stepping stone that lead me to the starting point of a thirty-five-year career in sales. At the time, I was twenty-one years old, and the J.T. Baker chemical representative for Stauffer had been promoted. My manager Wendy knew I was bored with lab work and wanted to get into the business side of things.

She told me there was a sales opening for the Pittsburgh territory, and that I should apply. I landed an interview that June, and it was a big deal. They flew me into Allentown from Pittsburgh, where I met with the Vice-President of sales. My desire for that job was strong, so I looked him in the eye and said, "If you give me a chance, I will knock your socks off!"

Well, I didn't get that job. They hired a guy based in Philadelphia. So, with determination, I got in my car with a briefcase and copies of my resume and drove into Pittsburgh, armed with a will to find another job. I met a guy on the street who was a headhunter. He offered me a job that was straight commission, and I took it. Now, understand that this meant no pay until I could make a placement. I worked the phones and made my first placement and commission check after six weeks.

When I got home that day, there was a message that J.T. Baker had called. I called them back, perplexed as to why they were calling. They offered me a position for the Eastern Pennsylvania territory based in Allentown: $22,700 plus commission and a company car. I would start on August 22, 1985. I would be selling salts, solvents, and acids. Success!

I was the very first woman in the company's eighty-five-year history to be hired for an outside sales position with no prior commercial sales experience.

The premise of the story is that there are possibilities and opportunities everywhere. Your potential is unlimited. Looking back on this, it was pure desire and decision that caused my success. I wanted more and I was an unconscious competent who experienced success. Your spirit grows, just like everything else in nature, always looking to expand and gain fuller expression. The behavior of truly living starts with a burning desire for more. The Bible says, "Blessed are those who are poor in spirit, they will inherit the earth." Being poor in spirit means you have a desire for more; you are not complacent.

If the desire is in your heart, you are meant to have it. Spirit is the movement. I was focused with clarity on what I wanted. I set a goal, made a committed decision, and jumped into action, willing to do whatever it was going to take to get there.

My desire, persistence, determination, and faith, caused my result, but I had no conscious awareness that I was following a recipe that I could follow at any time to generate the outcomes

I wanted. I did not realize at the time that my thoughts were enabling my results.

My intention in writing this book is to share what I have learned about applying the metaphysical laws of the universe, and the spiritual laws for success that allow you to sell more by understanding yourself and others. These laws occur effortlessly in nature, and they apply to selling. The laws tell us what professional selling is, and what it is not. When you are calibrated with universal law towards your joy you will win by law, not by luck. I hope my insight and stories provide you with a conscious awareness of how to recognize whether you are in alignment with universal laws of success while selling. By this understanding, the service you provide others will change the world's perception of what selling really is.

I've written this book for all professional salespeople, who endeavor daily to continually develop their character, who desire to become elite, powerful persuaders, and whose aim is to serve others and help them achieve what they want. I am also writing for those of you who are just beginning your sales career.

I've seen a lot of books about the mechanics of the sales process, but, after thirty-five years, I've found the wisdom to know that it's more important to study the principles.

The game of selling is ninety-five percent mindset and five percent mechanics. Mechanics judge everything by the limitations of past experiences. But the creative principle of life is thought. When you examine the principle of any problem, you can always find a solution. The more problems you solve, the more sales you will make. Selling with spirit is a behavior, a movement, a way of living.

Now, let's get into the spirit of selling!

Chapter I: The Maze of Misconceptions About Sales

Selling is not something you do TO someone, it's something you do FOR someone. – Zig Ziglar.

How do we properly understand a concept? We need to know what the concept is, and what it is not. Concepts are abstract ideas; an understanding retained in the mind from reason, experience, or imagination. Concepts are building blocks behind principles, thoughts and beliefs. The danger of a misconception is analogous to using a map of Boston to navigate through Philadelphia. If your concept is misguided, you'll end up getting lost. I don't want you to get lost.

Misconceptions about selling are commonplace, but we can clearly define selling: Selling is the process of understanding what a customer wants and helping them get what they want. Selling is guiding someone through a transformation. Selling is about serving the client and being compensated for the service. As we go through these misconceptions, I ask you to allow yourself the opportunity to do some re-evaluation. Do not ask if the concept is right or wrong, instead ask if the concept supports and serves you.

Misconception #1 – A salesperson is a con artist.

There is polarity in everything. Some of you reading this have positive impressions of salespeople, yet others have negative perceptions about salespeople. Why is that the case? Let's dive into the origin of the confluence of two words.

Think of a time when you saw something you wanted at the store, or perhaps you were invited to make an investment in yourself. As the salesperson approaches or concludes the presentation, you hear an inner voice saying, "Don't talk to her, she's just trying to sell you something," like it's a bad thing. That's your judge, your inner critic talking, not you. We will discuss the judge in a later chapter.

Or perhaps when you were a child you parents warned you to beware of strangers offering services. "Don't answer the door, or the phone, they're just trying to sell you something." You love and trust your parents so you accepted that idea. Maybe when you were six years old, in the store with your parents, you saw a toy you wanted. The salesclerk approached you, and your parents said, "Don't talk to him, let's go." So, you start to think there is danger in talking to salespeople.

Was that true fact or belief? Or perhaps your parents lacked the money and the heart to tell you *no*? Were they trying to divert your attention? Perhaps a close friend shared their belief with you about salespeople, and they questioned your career choice, "Why do you want to go into sales? All salespeople care about is making money." Ouch. Or perhaps you were hustled by someone and scolded by those close to you: "You can't trust salespeople."

What I am emphasizing is you make evaluations during your life based upon your awareness at the time. Sometimes we consciously think, and choose to accept, reject, neglect, or originate ideas. Other times we do not think; we either listen to our inner critic or accept what we hear to be true. If you want to succeed in sales, introspection on this topic is extremely beneficial; otherwise, your programming will hold you back from your unlimited potential.

If you have any negative perceptions about selling, understand this: ninety six percent of our behavior is habitual, on auto-pilot. Our perceptions, attitudes and belief govern our behavior. Perceptions shape our attitudes; they are the glasses through which we see and view our world. Perceptions are ideas emotionally impressed on our subconscious mind, and most of those accepted ideas came from people that have a strong pull on us. When we accept ideas to be true, they become our beliefs. A belief is like a computer program that operates on auto-pilot. The only way to change a perception or belief is to re-evaluate it.

Ask yourself, "What are my beliefs, perceptions, and attitude towards selling? Where did they come from? Do I defend them and if so, why? Does the belief empower me or hold me back? Which beliefs would help me to feel empowered and supported?"

Understand this: there is a confluence of words in peoples' minds that equates salespeople with con artists. The verb *sell* is defined as *to give or hand over in exchange for money; to persuade someone of the merits of something.* The prominent words in that definition are GIVE and PERSUADE. Let's take a look at those two words on a deeper level and stay in the verbs because that's where the action and the spirit is.

The definition of GIVE is *to freely transfer the possession of something to someone, to cause or to allow someone or something to have something, especially something abstract; to provide or supply with.* The definition of PERSUADE means *to cause someone to do something through reasoning or argument; to cause someone to BELIEVE something after sustained effort.* The underlying spirit of selling is based in giving, persuading, and transferring belief for acceptance of ideas. Everyone is selling something, to some degree, every day. For example, we sell ideas and values to our families to empower, support, or protect them. Those who pursue sales as a profession sell themselves, even as they sell products or services. They exhibit a positive mental attitude; they embrace their failures and learn from them. Salespeople continually raise their standards; true sales professionals set intentions to help you get what you want. Isn't that a positive thing? So, if selling is giving and persuading, what is the opposite?

The opposite is a con artist. A con artist is a person who cheats or tricks you by gaining your trust and persuading you to believe something that isn't true. A con artist perpetrates a hoax in order to GET something for themselves. So, both the con artist and the salesperson are persuaders; the key distinction is the intent behind the behavior; are they interested in getting or giving?

A con artist is self-centered and focused on what he or she will get from the transaction. A professional salesperson is service-centric and focused on helping you to get what you want. Sales professionals provide guidance, direction, and the bridge to get you to your promised land. They leave you with an impression of increase.

Take an inventory of what you've heard about salespeople, from all the people who have the most influence on you. I'm talking about mom, dad, spouses, partners, kids, and friends. Remember, their good intentions are based on their awareness.

With your new awareness and the distinction between con artist and professional salesperson, choose a belief that will empower you. Ask yourself, "Does my belief about selling and salespeople empower me? What ideas have I rejected, that perhaps I should accept? What ideas have I accepted that are not empowering and supporting me that I might reject? What would I need to notice, appreciate, or believe to be empowered to provide my sales services with enthusiasm? Now that you have the answer, accept the ideas that will empower you to get into the spirit of selling.

Misconception #2 – It Takes Pleasing Methods to make a sale

If you are new to sales, or just starting your own business and suffering from "approval addiction," you're probably looking for pleasing methods to sell your products and services. The other day, an entrepreneur said to me, "I don't want to be salesy.'" I said, "What does that even mean?"

There is one basic dislike common to all of us: we don't like to talk to people about things they may not want to discuss. However, we must realize that most humans are highly resistant to change, even when it's for their own good. If you suffer from approval addiction, that means you are concerned about what others think about you. Perhaps you fear rejection. When a customer puts up any resistance to what you're selling, they're resisting change. They are resisting the idea. Or perhaps what you have is not the perfect fit. If you think they're resisting you, and you will shut down and take it personally. If you suffer from approval addiction, you will fail to persuade them because of your desire to be appreciated and liked. You won't approach people unless you think they're looking for what you have. And so many people will miss out because you will lay judgement on them!

Albert E. N. Gray wrote about this topic in his speech, "The Common Denominator of Success." He pointed out that successful people focus on pleasing results, not pleasing methods. Successful people accomplish things they want to accomplish by doing things they don't like to do. Their purpose drives them. Successful people understand that they need to use their will and belief to build a bridge, so the client can see how to get from where they are to where they want to be—in their promised land. A salesperson who lacks confidence, will and belief, will fail to persuade clients. It's the salesperson's belief and enthusiasm that empowers the client's belief.

My favorite role model for persuasion is Saint Paul. Saint Paul had passion, and he was focused on results. When he was Saul, the Christians feared him. This was a man who got things done. He went from killing Christians as Saul, to converting people to Christianity as Paul with the spirit of passion. He knew his purpose, he was focused on pleasing results, and he wielded his belief and his will to serve others and bring them to the promised land. Purpose is what provides our spirit with joy and fulfillment. Purpose is not about you, it's about something bigger, that impacts people in a positive way. Look at yourself and what drives you. Find your purpose and write it down. Get into the spirit of "pleasing results" by having a purpose that is bigger than your basic needs. Purpose mixed with desire is the lever that will shift you into a gear you forgot you had and allow you to experience quantum leaps in your sales performance.

Let's examine pleasing methods versus pleasing results through the four basic habits that earn sales: contact, call, persuade, and work habits.

A sale does not begin until you contact someone. Who are you contacting? Are you only contacting those who express interest or are you also contacting those who could benefit from your service? If you focus on pleasing methods as you contact clients, you will limit opportunities. Think about the mission in commission. Who needs what you have? Spread the good news!

I challenge you to adopt the belief that it's easier to persuade contacts than it is to hunt for a person who wants what you have. Many people don't know they need your product until you talk to them. Think of the Christians' first sermons from the Acts of the Apostles. They contacted everyone and spoke in all languages. They didn't limit themselves to people who expressed an interest in Christianity. Yes, there were those in the crowd that were perplexed, confused, or skeptical, but they amazed and converted three-thousand people that day! Professional salespeople look for potential in all their contacts— to create sales or referrals.

Once you contact the customer, you need to get their attention. Ask yourself, whose attention am I getting? If you are calling customers based on whether you think they'll talk to you, you've fallen into a common first-timer trap. Yes, you want to make the sales call and practice your presentation, but if you fail to make presentations in front of people who are willing to do what you want them to do, you will be wasting your time. Let me provide an example.

I worked in the life science and diagnostics industries, selling products to people in biology, medical, or oncology research, and diagnostic testing labs. I witnessed many new sales representatives who suffered from approval addiction. First timers tend to call on lab technicians because they are easy to access. This is a good way to gather information about opportunities, but it typically doesn't result in a sale. The lab technicians don't get much attention, so they're willing to listen, would like to buy, and—they have no authority to buy. The real objective is to get the attention of the Principal Investigator, or the Lab Administrator, the person who owns the budget and can sign the approval to purchase.

The sales representative can check the box for making a sales call, but they fail to get in front of the person who can say *yes*. It might be scary to talk to the owner or the president-- someone you never met, someone with a big title, but the winners focus on getting to the buyer who can sign off on the funding or time to do what you want them to do. Winners know that if they get the attention of someone unwilling to listen, by being truly interested in that person, they will be able to persuade them to do something for their own good, they'll make a sale.

As for persuasion, it is all about intent. Intent is the starting point of the spirit of selling. Before you walk in the door, you should see that sale being made. You should have a committed objective to gain agreement that moves the sales process forward. Get in the habit of being determined to persuade, to love, and to lead, based on the client's desires. Remember this from the definition: if you use your will and hold belief long enough, the belief will transfer to the customer. The objective is for the customer to get what they want. You must take the role of the leader and the guide. Remember that the customers "reasons" for not crossing the bridge are based on the past. They will never get to the other side of the bridge if you don't help them see what their brand-new day looks like—a day with a problem solved. You want to lead them from their heart not their head. Feed their desires, align with their motives, and be determined to serve them with your belief - help them cross the bridge.

If you adopt *pleasing results beliefs* for contacting, calling, and persuading, the working habits will take care of themselves. The key is to be in touch with your purpose and sell heart to heart. There is no inspiration, courage, or happiness in pure logic. Don't take anything personally. It's not about you, it's about them. As Albert Gray says, get in the habit of doing the things failures don't like to do.

Misconception #3 – Sell Features

Sales professionals must understand what they really sell. Over the last thirty-five years, I have witnessed many organizations, entrepreneurs, and seasoned salespeople-- including myself—get focused on new technology and features and forgetting to ask, "What am I really selling? What is the outcome for the client?" True professionals must never forget this fundamental principle: people do not buy things; they buy based on the emotions they feel from buying things. That is what we call benefits.

Elmer Wheeler had it right when he stated, "Sell the sizzle, not the steak. People do not buy quarter inch drills because they want the drill. They buy the drill because they want quarter inch holes."

Think about it: if you are a realtor, what are you really selling? Most people will say the house; however, what you're really selling is protection of cash from inflation and shelter for a family to make a home. How will the customer feel in that home? Does the environment support the client's wants and desires? People buy their homes based on their emotions, how they feel in the house. Some want to see the sunrise from the kitchen, others want to see the sunset or an ocean view or city skyline. Some want a place for the kids to play and the dog to run, others want a close-knit community to meet more people. Yet how many times have you met a realtor who wants to tell you about all the features of the home?

If you're a travel agent, you are not selling plane tickets, hotels, and cruises; you are selling a memorable experience that the family will treasure. Coaches and mentors don't sell programs; they sell confidence, improved decision making, improved self-image, and order of the mind.

The pros know to ask themselves the deeper introspective questions: what do my services and product provide the client, and what is that really worth? Does it align with the client's personal or professional motives? You can't sell something to someone unless you know what their motives are. Put order in place for people where disorder exists. Remember that, and you will always make sales.

I was ignorant of this concept at my first job, just out of college. Roger McFillan, the VP of Sales and my first sales mentor, made sure that all his new recruits would come out of the dark and into the light.

My first two-weeks were spent in boot camp at the Holiday Inn in Bethlehem, Pennsylvania. We traveled back and forth to the Phillipsburg, New Jersey chemical plant and administrative office. The intention of the bootcamp was to ensure that rookies would get the concept of what we were selling and why. Roger wanted that principle drilled into our minds, so we could succeed. Joe Alessi ran the training sessions and Roger would stop in every day to put the fear of God in us, to make sure we were learning and applying the knowledge with roleplays. Apply the knowledge, use it, practice it.

J.T. Baker had two key differentiators. First and foremost, J.T. Baker was a basic manufacturer of salt and acid. When you bought from J.T. Baker, you bought from the source, and it was a consistent product. This was a key selling point. Other companies bought products from multiple raw material sources and resold it with their name on it. J.T. Baker supplied not only lab reagents, but also, "Process bulk Chemicals" used in the production of things like Kodak film, capacitors for the electronics industry, circuit board cleaning, carbons, silicas, and pharmaceuticals.

In training, we were taught the Xerox selling process, PSS, or Professional Sales Skills. Roger was adamant that we would become true Professionals. We learned about all the open probe questions to ask, questions about the importance of consistency, meant to minimize variation in experiments or production. We were also taught the importance of getting to all four legs of the chair, to make a sale and confirm reality. Translated, *get to all four legs* means to question and meet with all the important players: user buyers, technical buyers, economic buyers, and to look for an inside coach.

When you sit on a one-legged stool, you will fall; when you have all four legs, you have a solid foundation for a sale, something to sit on with confidence. Roger taught us how to be curious, to ask questions, and to dig for problems to solve. He would say, "Get the perspective from the mountain versus one perspective down in the trees, so you don't miss out spotting an opportunity."

The second differentiator was the SAF-T-DATA labeling system on our chemicals. In the 1980s, the Right to Know Act required MSDS sheets for all chemicals, and safety education for all workers in the chemical industry. The labeling system concept was designed with intent to share safety information. People think in images. The label system used colors, pictures, and numbers for fast visual recognition of hazards. J.T. Baker sales representatives offered free training on the system, which was a big hit with the safety officers at labs and production facilities. This service was an entrance strategy to get into new accounts, a way to find an inside coach. The SAF-T-DATA System label provided an advantage and a point of differentiation from our competitors. The benefit was training compliance for the employer, and ease of use and awareness for the employee handling the chemical. People loved the picture concept versus having to read a bunch of written words.

The biggest sale I made at J.T. Baker during my eight-year tenure was a six-figure contract for salt, and it was made in the spirit of this principle: know what you are selling. Cabot Corporation made carbons for capacitors and used potassium chloride in the manufacturing process. I found an inside coach and garnered his support after doing a free safety seminar. I asked questions to the people who worked at Cabot, and I found that they were having quality issues with their product. I also learned that they were having waste issues with raw materials because the salt containers in the plant would get wet due to rain.

Wet salt couldn't be used because it would introduce water into their chemical process. Their carbon was sold to make capacitors for electrical devices, and water in carbon has a negative effect on electrical conductivity, which in turn impacts the downstream quality of the capacitors. Long story short, we had similar waste issues at the J.T. Baker plant, from carboard barrel packaging that got wet in our warehouses. Since J.T. Baker sold salt to multiple customers in the electronics industry, the quality team converted the packaging for drums of salt from cardboard to blue poly containers. Those containers were waterproof and sealed tightly.

The procurement gentleman at Cabot was always shopping for the best price. The quality team was frustrated because they were losing business due to quality issues. The CEO was all over them to resolve the problem. They had multiple vendors for the raw materials. The vendors were not basic manufacturers, and they were having inventory waste from wet cardboard barrels of the raw material salts. These issues impacted their supply and turnaround time for product deliveries to their customers. Their reputation and financial profitability were hampered, and those problems were problems I could address.

I invited the quality manager, production manager, and procurement manger in for a plant tour and site visit. I closed the deal based on local domestic consistent supply: packaging, safety, and trust. I got a premium price; they paid more for the salt. But they were not buying salt. They were buying satisfaction felt from the relationships they built in the sales process. We provided solutions to their problems and gained their trust. Choosing J.T. Baker as their primary supplier allowed them to regain their reputation and financial profitability, also known as the motive.

Know what you are selling, and never attempt to start selling until you discover the customer's motive.

Misconception #4 – I need to make a sale.

Selling is all about creating value. Become a value creator and accept that idea. Every sales call requires a commitment objective: to gain an agreement with the client to move the sales process forward. A commitment objective is an intention for the call, and that is good. The key is to resist getting attached to a specific outcome. You might say to yourself, "Wait a minute, why would I not want to be fixed on making the sale?" And my answer is you do not make a sale, you receive it. Set an intention to cause the sale. Create so much value that they want to buy! Don't focus on the effect, receiving the sale. Have a mindset that embraces the unknown as a playful game. Instead of thinking about how to get the sale, use all your power to think about how you can create and give immense value to your client.

In sales, you can never be certain what you are walking into. It's like watching the pros play golf. Their objective is to stay present in the game and focus on the next shot. You will benefit by doing the same If your focus is on the prize, the outcome, and not the next shot, you are not in the moment where your power is. Selling is leading, guiding, and creating value; being ready for any and all situations. Many new to sales get thrown off course by expecting a certain response and getting something unexpected. Because salespeople are not prepared to dance with the unknown, they react rather than respond. Customers remember the sales professionals who are in the moment with them. They can feel the ones who are not present. It's not about you, it's about meeting your client where they are and helping them to get to where they want to go.

When the unexpected happens, the trick to staying in charge is to use your power instead of force. Power is connection, force is separation. If you believe you "have to" sell your products or yourself "to" people to "get" income for your business, you will be coming from a place that will have you working in complete opposition to the principle of natural law. "Have to" is coming from the space and illusion of separation. Force is the presence of fear, a sure sign you are trusting in your own strength, denying the presence of a higher power, that you are relying on your own power to feel safe.

Force and fear show up when you are separated; you don't rely on any help from the universe, and you are not in the present, not leaning into the customer's circumstance and looking for ways to add value. Often, we become impatient, and we don't trust the outcome. The inner talk may sound like this: *How is this going to look? I need my commission now. If I don't get this sale, I will lose the bonus I was counting on. Am I going to be fired? Management just doesn't understand. Why isn't my team getting the real story? Why did we forecast this?*

Be aware that our desire to control the outcome stems from a lack of faith in the Universe and ourselves to deliver in the timeframe we want, or from our fear that something bad will happen. We tie the outcome to our happiness and safety. When we do this, we lose sight of a plan beyond our own. If you've been here, realize the cause is the lack of confidence. Build your confidence up. Don't be the wave that decides to take on the ocean. Get into the spirit of the game. The opportunities to add value are there if you actively look for them.

In Major League Baseball, an ace is the starting pitcher who is meant to pitch at least five innings to help the team win the game. I like to remember this five-letter acronym, AACEE, to remind myself of ways to create value, the non-monetary value that matters. When you create meaningful relationships with humanity, you will reap in a non-linear fashion, and the returns will be exponential.

The first A is Attention. Energy grows where your attention goes. Am I paying attention to details, following up, checking in before and after the sale for satisfaction? Am I providing the best possible service?

The second A is Appreciation. People go where they are appreciated. The gift of appreciation is finding the good in others and acknowledging it. It can be their smile, their humor, their enthusiasm, their knowledge, or their creativity. The more you appreciate others, the more *you* appreciate in value. When we forget to appreciate others, we depreciate. Appreciation of others is key to increase your value and worth.

The C is Consistency. Can my customer count on the same quality experience, no matter how uncertain times are? Have you ever met a salesperson who came across as forceful and left you with a bad perception? Observe this behavior at the end of a quarter, when the CEOs and managers are under high pressure to meet revenue targets and have fallen behind their forecast. Instructions are given to the sales force to "make" it happen, instead of the instruction to create more value the customer wants to buy. Stress gets triggered and customers experience reactive behavior instead of responsive behavior. Customers are drawn toward sales professionals who are consistent with their character, salespeople who provide value, regardless of the circumstances.

The first E is empathy. Put yourself in the other person's shoes. Understand the person you are talking to and what their perspective is. How does it feel? When we connect with another on an emotional level, we form a composite (or mastermind) with the person, so we can help them build a bridge to where they want to go, by first understanding where they are. We are on the same side of the table for a win-win. There are many books on this topic of Emotional Intelligence. People buy based on their emotions; on the feeling they will get from the experience. Empathy is foundational for problem solving. I use the acronym CEC (Continuing Educational Credits) to remind myself to serve my clients with empathy. Cognitive empathy:

what would I be thinking if this happened to me; Emotional empathy: *I had a similar situation and I recognize the feeling from my own experience*; and Compassionate Empathy: *what action can I take to serve this person?*

The second E is Excellence. What am I bringing to the party? What is my attitude? Our attitudes are the energy we project on others. Often, we mirror others. If someone is nice to us, we are nice back. The question is, will you give everyone a 10 out of 10, regardless of their attitude toward you? Jesus put it well when He said, *"I say unto you, love your enemies; bless them that curse you; do good to them that hate you; pray for them that despitefully use you."* I didn't understand what he meant until recently. By law, if you extend a loving thought to another, you remove the opposition in your consciousness so you will not attract it anymore. The highest good in you can only attract the highest good of another. The Master understood the Law of Non-resistance well. Excellence is about raising your standards, the quality and quantity of service you provide. The more often you raise standards, the more your value increases.

Your power is being a giver, a value creator. Recognition of how to adjust yourself to work *with* the circumstance by acceptance, internal adjustment, and looking for opportunities to create value, will put you in the spirit of selling, a spirit to win the game. Focus on value creation and expect to receive a sale. Be open to receiving from multiple sources. The sale may not always come from where you created value, but it will come; it's the law. It is knowing that if you are giving and serving others with the use of your talents, the good must come back to you—it is law.

Misconception #5 – Selling is only for the sales department

Everyone on this planet is selling something. It's the circulation system of life, and certainly the circulation system for the marketplace. Kids sell their parents to get what they want. Spouses sell each other on what is needed to run the household, or what vacations to take first. When you are seeking a job and go on an interview, you are selling the employer on you. When you meet the man or woman of your dreams and date, or start looking for that person, you are selling yourself.

Selling is a natural form of existence. It's the process of serving one another, no different than how the body works. The heart delivers blood with oxygen to the organs, the liver provides detox services, the eyes provide sight, ears provide sound, the immune system provides protection against disease. Everyone has a gift, talent, or service to provide.

So why is it that many organizations think selling is only for the sales department? Yes, the sales department is deployed to make the contacts, the calls, and to persuade and close sales. But the selling doesn't end with the commencement of a sale, it's just the beginning. Growth happens from momentum, building a customer base, keeping it, and gaining referrals.

In the marketplace, money is exchanged for value and benefit. It is cash that provides the oxygen to keep the organization alive. The higher the value and benefit, the more money can be exchanged. The marketplace is dynamic, always changing, which means that opportunities for creating order where disorder exists are present in abundance, especially if you're looking for them. Here is my point: there are two mindsets an organization can adopt. The first mindset is *everyone in the organization is in sales or sales support.* The second mindset is *selling is only for the sales department.* Which mindset do you think sees more opportunities to serve and solve problems?

Entrepreneurs and business owners must understand their why, their purpose for being in business. Who are they serving, what experience are they creating, and how will they continue to grow and expand? From purpose comes the plan of how to get the product or service to the right people, people who will benefit from the value, and how the value can be continually increased. Last, what problem are you solving to bring order where disorder exists, and what is that worth to a client?

The mindset of an organization creates the culture. Look at Apple, Disney, Amazon—the organizations that thrive through all types of market disruptions. As Simon Sinek would say, *they have an infinite mindset.* The spirit of selling is a powerful mindset for leaders and employees to adopt. If everyone in the organization understands the why, the how, and the what, and continually looks for opportunities to solve new problems, the organization will thrive and evolve to play an infinite game. Selling is value creation; it is not limited to the sales department.

Chapter II: Do you Judge Money or Expect It?

Jesus said unto him, "Thomas, because thou hast seen Me,

thou hast believed. Blessed are they that have not seen and yet

have believed." - John 20:29

When you think about it, most things in life are invisible. Energy is invisible, yet it is everywhere. Money is no exception.

School teaches us how to account for money but fails to teach all the concepts about what it is, how to earn it, where it comes from, and how it works. A fundamental natural law is at work and those who understand the law will never be stressed about money.

Selling is not about the money. Money is a result of good selling. When you become really good at solving people's problems and creating order where disorder exists with the product or service you provide, you will have an abundance of money as your reward. The trick is to see money as your servant; make it work for you instead of chasing it. Stop blocking yourself from receiving it. Since these money concepts can be either judgement or expectation, it deserves some introspection.

All businesses rely upon their sales teams to generate cash flow. Cash is the oxygen that keeps the business vibrant and alive. The money concepts you accept cause your results. The last thing you want to have as a sales professional are disempowering concepts about money that block the flow of cash.

Now let's debunk the most common misconceptions and societal myths about money.

Money Misconception #1 – You make money.

It's funny how many times you hear people say they need to make money; they don't understand that money is not made, it is earned. The mint makes money, you earn money. Look closely at the distinction between the words "make" and "earn." One is a form of bartering; a bushel of wheat for a pair of shoes. The other is a form of investment. Investments create lasting wealth and are in alignment with universal law. Money is currency and currency is energy. Money has been part of the human experience for over 3000 years. Money's value is symbolic and allows people to trade goods and services indirectly. Trade is finite, investment is infinite. You make the investments; money is your return on investment, your earnings.

Money Misconception #2 – Money comes and money goes.

You may have heard people say, "Money comes and money goes." But have you ever wondered why? What causes it to come? Money comes where it is cared for and put to use. It does not want to be idle. That's why they say the best measure of your financial health is your net worth as opposed to your annual income.

Why does it go away? Energy is always circulating and expanding. When circulation and expansion are cut off, or restricted the flow stops. Money, like energy, wants to circulate and expand. Too often, people hold onto their money, in fear that they will run out or they spend it instead of investing it. Spending and hoarding behaviors lack alignment with principles for circulation, expansion or investment. As a result, money is repelled. When a branch is cut from the vine that gives it the energy of life to grow and expand, it dies.

Money Misconception #3 – Money comes from people and organizations.

Money is currency, and currency is energy. It doesn't come to you from someone or something; you attract it from inside you, from what you become, from your value and the value you create for others. The more people you positively impact, the more energy expands and comes back to you.

Have you ever observed an employee expecting a raise without doing anything extra first to earn it? That employee is displaying their ignorance of the law of compensation. You will never earn more than what you are being paid unless you do more, create more value, than what you are being paid to do.

Want more? Decide what you are willing to give or give up to get it. Release more energy!

Money comes through people or organizations, not from them. The misconception that trips us up is expecting a result to come from where we left our contribution. Have you ever heard someone say, "I gave so much to (fill in the blank), but didn't get anything back from (fill in the blank)?"

There is a difference between the idea of trading and giving. Trading is a linear exchange; giving is non-linear exchange. To give is to release without attachment. And yet, we graciously know that receiving is to be expected, and that we must be open to receiving. Trading is an exchange of goods or services between two entities. Trading is giving to get something.

Too often I see people who long for prosperity living with the limiting belief that their trade is lopsided. They look at their circumstance, who they are employed by, for example, and only see reasons why they can't get what they want. They give up. You will hear them say, "What's the point?" It's like watching people put themselves in their own prisons. The only problem here is ignorance.

Money doesn't come from an employer. Money may come *through* an employer, or an unexpected source, but it comes because of the value you create in yourself or the value you create for others. You become more. You increase the value of YOU Inc; you do more than what you are being paid for; you become more, so your stock value goes up. If your current employer does not recognize your value, someone else will. Money is the effect; YOU are the cause.

In the book *The Science of Getting Rich* by Wallace Wattles, Wallace talks about doing things in a certain way. He writes, "Always give a use value greater than the cash value you take." Jim Rohn says, "Work more on yourself than you do on your job." These men understood the principle that we all have the ability to become prosperous. The only thing holding us back is ignorance. Money comes through people, not from them.

Your mind is like a plot of land. You are the creator of your life. Let's use the analogy of a gardener planting wheat seeds in the garden to explain where the money comes from. One wheat seed, if planted and nourished in an environment where it can unfold, will produce a live plant with five bushels on the stock. That wheat stock generates 125,000 new seeds. Now, if you were to cut open the seed before you plant it, you wouldn't find 125,000 seeds, right? Where does the abundance of seeds come from? Nature does its part!

Likewise, if you do nothing with the seed, you do not gain a harvest. If you place an acorn in your coat pocket it will not grow into an oak tree. The take home lesson we can learn from nature is that we cannot get something for nothing. Make the investment first, then expect a return. It's the law of sowing and reaping. Ask yourself daily, "How can I increase my service, give more, become more?" Then act on those ideas and let nature do her part. Nature will do her part in a non-linear fashion, and you will always reap more than you sow. Money is energy that grows and goes to where it is appreciated. You are the cause; money is the effect. Want more money? Become more and allow nature to do her part! Accept the idea to receive from both expected and unexpected sources.

Money Misconception #3 – Hard and honest work is the only way to create wealth

My grandparents came over to the United States through Ellis Island. All four of my grandparents believed in hard honest work, that it would be rewarded. We certainly learned to embrace the work ethic and never expected something for nothing. I always wanted more, and expected I had to do all the work, that no one or nothing would make it happen if I did not cause it. That was the root of my misunderstanding. I thought I was generating the energy by my work; what I really was doing was directing and releasing the energy. The prayer of St. Francis lays out the truth – "Lord make me an instrument of your peace…" The key word is instrument. The Universe, Divine Providence, the power, God, or whatever you want to name it is the source. You and I are the instruments.

Here's the deal - there are only two ways to earn money. People at work and Money at work. Unfortunately, most people are employing only one of two strategies, trading their time for money, people at work, under the belief that hard work will come through and deliver. The real question is who delivers?

I believed in hard work but it came with a ton of stress because I thought I was the only source to rely upon. The problem with the hard work belief is the separation illusion. Hard work is a linear idea, and if that is the only one you have you are limited.

There are new non-linear ideas that you can evaluate and accept to multiply your effectiveness and not have to go it alone. One of those new ideas is to allow the universe to do her part. The money is coming from the Universe to you. You've never been alone.

The reason the masses believe it takes hard work to create wealth is because the masses haven't realized their connection and oneness with Infinite Intelligence. When you think you are alone and you can't get what you want, you experience fear. That's what restricts the flow. And when fear sets in, you cannot hear your intuition.

Why do you think humanity has a tendency to drift into self-centeredness? Because they believe in the illusion of separation. How often do you think about yourself versus thinking about others? For me, it is a constant tug of war, but I am grateful now that I can see myself drift and catch it more quickly. If I can learn, you can learn. When we are in a state of being self-centered, we cut off our connection to the whole. Of course, being by yourself would be hard – but why would you want to live in that illusion? Self-centeredness results in becoming tight from fear. Where fear exists, intuition will not operate. The flow is constricted. To feel intuition and hear it, one needs to be relaxed, open, and present.

So, it's the end of the quarter, your big order is delayed due to some objection. The pressure is on to deliver – so what do you do? Most of the time we give ourselves the answer instead of patiently waiting to receive it. A sense of urgency is critical but are you embracing it by force or with your power?

The more we tap into the identity of the wealth we desire, acting as if we have it already—because we do in our imagination—the more answers we will receive. Intuition is significantly stronger than reason. The Universe communicates to you through intuition, a feeling that puts you into motion. Love is stronger than logic. Intuition will never fail you. Learn to relax, listen, and receive it.

I adopted a habit Earl Nightingale suggested from his course and book called Lead the Field. This new habit allowed me to develop my faith in a higher power, my intuition, and to mine that power daily—like mining for gold to sell more. I learned how to give up the idea I had to do it alone; I learned to give up the attachment and control.

Here's the idea: It takes five hours a week. Given we sleep eight hours, work eight hours, and have eight additional hours to do with as we wish, I decided to invest one of my extra hours, five days a week, for this: I got an idea journal.

Monday through Friday, I ask myself these questions:

"How can I increase my quality and quantity of service?"

"What else would my customers love?"

"How can I become more effective and take my standards to the next level?"

All I have to do is relax and listen for the answers.

Once you realize and accept the idea that the higher power is infinite—infinite in you, and infinite in everyone, life becomes easy and effortless. Our job is to love and give—and that's EASY. Adopt this philosophy to bust up fixed habit patterns in a relaxed and focused way. Everything in life is "made for you," not "done to you." Ask yourself, "What is the gift?" Make the decision that earning money is EASY. Tap into your intuition on a daily basis. Prayer is your goal; intuition is the source to answer your prayer. Ask for what you want daily, and ask how it can be easy. Remember, everything you believe is true. Trust in the power. Remember you are not alone – you are the instrument who directs the power.

Ask and it will be given to you; seek and you will find; knock and the door will be opened to you. – Matthew 7:7

Money Misconception #4 – Money is bad and unimportant.

Do you feel repulsion, critical, or judgmental when you hear people talk about loving money, like that's a bad thing? Would you feel the same way if someone was talking to you about loving their grandkids?

Let's eliminate this myth. There is nothing bad about money. Money is energy, and something we receive in return for our value creation. It is a symbol of our freedom to be, do, have, and give. It is a reflection of how much service we have provided. Money allows us to create life on our terms, for the harmonious good of all concerned.

We've been highly trained to love grandkids, and yet told it is not okay to love the symbol of our freedom. The truth is, we can be financially prosperous and be deeply spiritual when we carefully examine our beliefs and choose what we want to believe about money. We can welcome money into our life. If we realize that money is the effect of producing much good for others, then we can look at wealth and the wealthy in a different light.

Money has caused betterment in the world, not harm. It is money that provides shelter, pays for clothing, education, transportation, vacations, family get-togethers, money that supports philanthropic causes. It is the exchange mechanism or currency that causes the marketplace to thrive. Money was created as a replacement for the bartering system. Can you imagine if you had to physically exchange goods to acquire the things you need?

So where did the thoughts of money being bad or unimportant come from? The three most common mindsets responsible for blocking our abundance and judging money are:

1) *The "GET" mindset stemming from lack or scarcity; this mindset puts the attention on the glass that is half empty versus being half full.*

2) *Fear of loss and lack of belief in a power greater than ourselves. Universal abundance does not exist in unbelief. Worry and doubt will rob you of belief, and statistics show that 92% of what people worry about are things that never happen. These worries take up value time, cause mental anguish and stress, and are absolutely unnecessary.*

3) *The "I am not enough" or "I am powerless"*
mindset. When I went to coaching school, this
mental block was what we called a gremlin. I'm not
smart enough, skilled enough, educated enough, too
young, too old etc. It is comparison versus
inspiration; competitive thinking versus creative
thinking.

These negative mindsets cut off our connection to our freedom and cause money to flee because it is not accepted. The best way to evaluate your money beliefs is to ask, where did this idea come from? Is it serving me to help me get what I want? If not, try this idea on: Money is good, money is important, and you can be, do, have and give more when you have it. Use this affirmation: *Up until now, I let fear, scarcity, and comparison rule my mind, but now I control my mind and I love money, the symbol of my freedom*! Love is the attraction power.

Money Misconception #5 – *It is better to give than to receive.*

The number one reason people do not reach their full potential is that most people are poor "receivers." Why? Conditioning and self-worth are two big reasons. How often have you heard the masses state it is better to give than to receive? Have you ever noticed that the people who propagate that idea are people and groups who want you to give to them, so that they will receive? The danger of that idea is it leaves no room for you to be ready to graciously receive.

Giving and receiving are two sides of the same coin! For every giver, there must be a receiver, and for every receiver, there must be a giver. If you are not willing to receive, you are "robbing" those who want to give to you. Have you ever tried to give someone a compliment and they refuse to say thank you? It sucks, right? Instead of feeling good when they say thank you, you feel terrible. Giving and receiving are equal in importance.

The law of sowing and reaping states that whatever you put out you will get more of, so why would you not expect to receive? The most common answer is self-worth. Being worthy or unworthy is a belief we attach to ourselves. It's all a made-up story. Babies are not born with stamps on their heads that say "worthy" or "unworthy." All human beings were created for greatness. Our greatest assets are the mind and our word. It's what makes us different than the animals, unless you're watching Dr. Doolittle where the animals talk. When used properly, we can create a life with joy and fulfillment that is effortless.

So why do we feel unworthy? A good question to ask yourself is, who decides your worth? Are you in the habit of letting others decide your worth? If so, why did you give your power away? Self-image controls the "giving" and self-worth controls the "receiving." What you receive is what you allow. I remember going on my first manager job interview, and I did not receive the promotion. A younger gentleman named Jon got that job, and I couldn't figure out why. I thought all my giving would be recognized. I did not go into that interview expecting to come out with a promotion, I was hoping for it; there is a difference between hope and expectation. In retrospect I realize it was my self-worth that held me back. It was a blessing and lesson I had to learn. Jon's high self-worth rubbed off on me while I reported to him, and I ended up receiving the promotion to District Sales Manager within a year under his tutelage; Jon recommended me for the job. I received that promotion because I believed I was worthy, and I graciously received it.

Misconception #6 – You must not spend today, or you will not have money in the future

Now is all there ever is. If we adopt the belief that we cannot use money in the now, we cut off the opportunity to use it for our good, or for someone else's good, in the present. It's like having the water shut off to our home. Abundance cannot be in the present with that belief. Abundance is infinite, but goes where it is welcomed. There is also a difference between the meaning of spend versus invest. To invest is to expect a meaningful reward. To spend is to use up or exhaust, not expecting to receive anything back. Saving money for your future by investing it is a prudent measure of reason because you are showing care and thought for your future.

This is a great example of the choice and power of words. "Do not, will not, and spend" are not very empowering expansive words. These words block abundance. When you examine your money beliefs and paradigms, pay close attention to the words and where you picked up and accepted the idea. Was it an idea you originated, or one you inherited? Does it empower you in the present? If not, what would empower you? Allow yourself to accept new ideas and reject the ones that no longer empower you. Perhaps a better belief could be stated by saying, "I always have the money I need, when I need it because I carefully invest it." Take an inventory of your money beliefs, and remember, a belief is nothing more than an evaluation. Evaluate your assumptions and beliefs. Choose them consciously. You may not have been responsible for putting those beliefs in your mind, but you are responsible to change them if they don't serve you and your potential.

Misconception # 7 – I earn money for my time.

Do you think you get paid based on your results, or based upon your time? Have you ever heard this advice? "Go to school, get good grades, a good job, and steady paycheck?" Many people take that advice because it's all they hear. You are in sales, and my guess is, if you are good at it, you choose sales as a career. You are confident in your performance and ability to produce the results. You are more interested in the incentive program than you are in the salary. Why? Steady pay checks typically interfere with your ability to earn what you are worth.

I would like to ask your permission for me to say something direct. If you do not have this confident mindset to be paid on results, it is likely you are a security seeker who is afraid—afraid that you will not be able to earn enough based on your performance; you settle for earning just enough to survive, just enough to be comfortable.

My mentor states it like this: selling is the highest paid profession in the world. Why? Because it's a results-based business. Those who produce the biggest results garner the biggest rewards. Salespeople who believe in themselves, their value, and their ability to create value, deliver that value.

There are three ways to earn money. One is to trade your time for it. This is what the masses do. This is the typical forty-year plan followed by retirement, and it's what gets taught as the standard way in school. The problem with this strategy is that, sooner or later, you run out of time. If money is the symbol of our freedom, and we want more freedom, it pays to look at the other non-linear strategies. The second way to earn money is to invest money for money, like the money you invest in a 401K for your financial future: investments, annuities, real estate, dividend stocks. The third way is to have multiple sources of income where you're paid based on results. Examples of this include a salary with incentive plan, real estate investments, a network marketing opportunity, or writing a book. You can have many sources of income, and the key is that these multiple sources of income multiply your effectiveness, and help you earn money while you sleep! These sources multiply your impact to serve and produce results for hundreds or thousands of people.

The take-home message here is to choose an empowering habit. You are either in the habit of savings some of your earnings, spending all your earnings, or spending more than you earn. Saving money is investment, in alignment with natural law. Saving money allows you the opportunity to develop a mix of strategies for passive and active income streams later in life. It's never too late to save. Put your money to work and earn money based on results. People buy results, not time and you get paid based upon results.

Misconception # 8 – What you see is what you get.

When it comes to money, the masses think from their senses, focusing their attention on what they see in their bank account versus focusing their attention towards what they can create using their mental faculties.

Take the money focus test. Do you make decisions to buy based on what you have, or based upon what on you want and love? Do you want to become someone who creates whatever you set your mind to, or someone who settles for what you can get? Do you create or compete? These are good questions to ponder.

Consider this: the money you have now is an effect and direct correlation to the quantity and quality of service you have rendered up until this point. You caused what you have today, and you can cause something different if you don't like what you have. You have the power. Earning money is a habit of creating and investing. What are you in the habit of doing, and if you do not like your results, are you willing to change?

When we change, the effect changes; it's not the other way around. Settling is a choice. Settling is rationalizing and it sounds like this: "I want (fill in the blank) but..." Or, "I can't (fill in the blank) because I don't have..." Or, "I will (fill in the blank) as soon as..." You can have excuses or results. You settle when you make decisions based on what you have; you are focused on effect, not cause. You are stuck in a pattern of resistance.

But get this as well, your belief is serving you in some way. Perhaps it allows you to stay comfortable or stay in the shadows; or if you suffer from approval addiction, it allows you to feel part of the crowd. Einstein said that insanity is doing the same things over and over again and thinking the result will change.

Creation works through our transformation. Opportunity for financial success is without limit unless you are unwilling to create and invest. Creation is choosing courage over conformity.

Sales professionals create. The setback becomes the set up; the stumbling block becomes the stepping stone. By being non-resistant and in agreement with all that is prosperous, we use every means available to make it easy for prosperity to enter our lives. Our desire is lit. Our self- reliance and self-confidence will soar. When we take responsibility to cause our lives, to change how we show up, the effect changes; it is not the other way around. Start creating and investing and watch the money show up! Opportunity is infinite. What you see is a result of past thinking.

Chapter III: Know the rules and Get Into the Game!

"There's a difference between knowing the path and walking the path." – Morpheus

Playing the game of life is fun when you understand the rules of the game. The rules and principles for the game of life are universal and never change. Selling operates under these principles, as well. Divine Mind, Energy, God, has a vibration that is called Universal Law. When we operate in perfect rhythm and harmony with "law," the Universal Mind, we have access to our inner power and potential to co-create anything we want for the harmonious good of all concerned.

Many have written about Universal Intelligence vibration and I have studied these laws in depth over the last eighteen months. This understanding prompted me to write this book and relate the laws to selling. There are the seven universal laws for life, science, and nature. There are seven spiritual laws of success for humanity that apply to the necessity of dealing with people and being where the people are. These laws are predicated upon the concept that hard work is not the cause of success alone; success is the understanding of human nature. And there are two fundamental biblical laws. These three sets of laws are interwoven and here, I believe, to bring order and harmony for the greater good of all concerned. I may have heard of these concepts before, but prior to 2021, I had never put the puzzle together in such a way that would reveal the game rules and blueprint for successful living and selling. I had to understand these laws are interdependent. It's like studying the seven individual colors of light that make up the whole rainbow. The completeness of that understanding has carried me to find my pot of gold, my continual increased awareness.

I now know, at a conscious level, why I experience success in sales, and why I experienced failure during different periods of my career. I wrote this book to share the game rules and real-life sales stories that exemplify working in alignment with these laws—or in mis-alignment with law. There is a difference between being an unconscious competent and a conscious competent. The difference is awareness.

When you encounter a problem in selling do you review core principles or do keep using the mechanics that worked in the past? When the pandemic changed the rules for selling in 2020, restricting the amount of live, in person visits, did you lean into principle to adjust quickly?

My intent is to share with you a winning strategy for selling that will last a lifetime so you become a conscious competent professional salesperson. The premise of this book is to learn to sell by law not by luck. Use this chapter as your reference guide. The promise is, with study and application, you will gain an understanding that eliminates worry and doubt.

Universal Law Before we get into those stories, permit me to introduce you to the laws. Let's start with the seven natural laws of this universe. Since it's the universe we live in, we should understand how it works. Our universe is predicated on one fact; "Energy is." Science studies outside forces; theology studies inside forces. I have come to believe they are one and the same.

The Law of Perpetual Transformation. We become what we think about. Thought is energy. Energy is everywhere. Thought projected on this formless energy produces matter in the physical world. Energy moves into and out of form, from non-physical thought to physical form. The first law of thermodynamics states energy can neither be created or destroyed. It just is. The second law of thermodynamics states entropy is always increasing, everything is always moving toward a state of disorder. This is good for selling because there will always be a need to provide order where order does not exist. Order gets orders!

Just like water has three forms, gas, liquid, and solid; and moves back and forth between those forms, we operate in the same way: the spiritual plane is our spirit, our essence; the intellectual plane is our Mind, and Mind is movement; and the physical plane is brought into existence through the creation process with order (alignment with law) and movement (applied faith.) The spiritual and intellectual planes are invisible. Creation by man occurs from the inside out, from the invisible to the visible physical plane. Real advances in our physical world have always come from ideas and dreams formed in the imagination, ideas that the inventors fell in love with. Their desire was emotionally strong, and they decided to make their desire a reality, to let themselves become the person they had to become to bring the dream into reality. Those three steps-- accept, decide, and let—caused everything these inventors needed to be attracted to them. Examples include Walt Disney, Steve Jobs, Thomas Edison, Henry Ford, Charles Schwab, Martin Luther King, Marie Curie, and many others.

Perpetual transmutation is the creation process. In selling, we seek to truly understand our clients' needs and mastermind with them for ways to create value in their imagination and ours. It's a partnership of creativity that helps solidify the sale. If we succeed at getting the client emotionally involved with the idea, so they can make a decision to get what they want, the effect will be a sale. In summary, human beings are designed to create from the invisible, from the inside out. Einstein put this law in a scientific equation, $e = mc2$; energy and mass are interchangeable.

Spirit of Selling (S.O.S.) tip – *Be present with your client in the NOW and focus on what can be versus what is. Co-create value with the client by forming and emotional composite in their imagination. Remember people buy based on how the feel, they justify their decision with logic.*

The Law of Vibration and Attraction. Everything in life is energy, including your thoughts and your actions. Energy vibrates at a frequency. You and I are balls of energy, and there are infinite numbers of frequencies that we can tune and thereby fully resonate. We use the word "feeling" to describe our vibration or radio channel, and since like attracts like, we attract everything in our life based upon our vibration. Your radio station is always on – there is no "off" switch. We control our vibration just like a radio dial, based upon what we think and what actions we take. Your vibration in your physical form is a reflection of the impression of your thoughts, feelings, and actions, also known as your Attitude, your energy field. How you show up matters. The key word is impression. Whatever you are emotionally involved in and believe is impressed, causing your vibration frequency. Your radio station is always on and you have the power to adjust your frequency with your inner tuner which has two parts that must be fused together; Desire and Expectation. Desires or Prayers are answered in accordance to belief. You cannot fool principle but you can fool yourself. Desire is the request; belief activates the power of attraction.

Let's go back to Walt Disney. When he got emotionally involved with the idea of Disneyland, his frequency changed. He acted as if it was already so, and from that vibration, he attracted all that was necessary to bring Disneyland to life. When you go into a sales call, think about what invisible feeling you are transmitting to the client—the client will pick up on your vibration—and make sure you are on the channel to serve them powerfully.

• • •

S.O.S. tip – _Attitude matters, it's how you show up. Put yourself on a channel to serve your clients powerfully. Your vibration precedes manifestation! Decide to bring your 10 out of 10 regardless of how any client treats you or whatever circumstance you face. Expect the sale before you make the call. Know that no matter what the outcome, you will be leaving them with an impression of increase and what you put out, will come back to you. It's law._

The Law of Relativity. Nothing is what it is until you relate it to something. Everything in life is relative by comparison. Energy just is. There are always greater and lesser degrees of comparison. We create our reality in the NOW by our vibrational stance. The Law of Relativity can either empower you or disempower you, it is simply a matter of choice. Decide to use relativity to empower you. Remember, our perception or point of view is based upon how we relate and what we relate it _to_. What will make you feel good? We get to choose how to relate one experience or thing to another unless we give our power away. Nothing is good or bad unless we say it is. It's not what you are exposed to that causes your reality, it is your interpretations. A good question to ask yourself is, *Compared to what? What am I comparing this to? Does it empower me? How would someone else see this? What else can I compare it to? What comparison puts me in a good vibration?*

S.O.S. tip - When you are selling, watch your attitude. Your perception is unique to you. Contrast helps you choose. Be a deliberate creator of value. Observe and cooperate instead of comparing and competing based on the IS-NESS of the present. Wayne Dyer said it best, "When you change the way you look at things, the things you look at change."

The Law of Polarity. Everything has an opposite; up and down, back and forth, right and left, etc. There are two sides to one coin. In the absence of that which you are not, that which you are...is not. It's the polar opposites that make existence possible. Everything in life has duality, oneness. It is the contrast that allows you to deliberately choose to experience life to the fullest and truly appreciate all that is in your world. Therefore, do not condemn, criticize, or complain about what you do not want or what you are not. Instead focus on the good, what you want in people and situations. Both are there; it's the way life is. Your empowerment is based upon where you place your focus and what you assume. Positive assumptions cause your heart to open and join. Negative assumptions cause your heart to close and separate. What you focus on will be enlarged in your life.

> *S.O.S. tip:* *If you are going to make an assumption in sales, always focus on the positive side. Use your persuasion skills to keep your clients focused on the positive. A higher vibration will always knock out a lower vibration and allow for more creativity. Take your power back and direct your focus. Seek to find the good in every situation. Whatever you seek, you shall find. Nature, Spirit, Life is always moving toward the positive pole and you will be wise to do the same.*

The Law of Cause & Effect. Emerson referred to this law as the *law of laws*. Think of a boomerang or reciprocity; whatever you put out will come back to you. It's Newton's third law: for every action there is an equal and opposite reaction. It's the Law of Sowing and Reaping. Every cause has an effect, and every effect has a cause. A sale is the effect of the value you create; the cause for the sale is YOU, the value of YOU, and the value you create for your clients. Your value is increased when you always give more in *use value* than you what you take. Your value is the result of the standards you hold for yourself. The value you create is in direct proportion to the quantity and quality of service you provide. The more people you impact, the more value you create. Multiplication will create bigger leaps in performance than addition.

> *S.O.S. tip:* *Remember YOU are the cause; the sale is the effect and so is your commission. Want more? Examine your personal standards and keep refining your craft. Serve more people powerfully; Assume the feeling of the wish fulfilled. Ask yourself how can I give more? Serve more people? Multiply my efforts? Create more value and always follow the golden rule. Treat others as you want to be treated. Leave everyone you meet with an impression of increase. The sale may or may not come back directly from where you added value, it may come from a*

referral or at a later time, but know it will come back to you. It's

the law.

The Law of Rhythm. Energy operates on frequencies, which are waves. Waves are non-linear. Night follows day, day follows night. The pendulum of life is always swinging. Frequencies and waves have peaks and valleys to create pitch, contrast, intervals, and dynamics which is an element of linear ordering. The secret to the Law of Rhythm is to begin to trade expectations for appreciation. You always know what you will give up but you never know what you will gain. There are four seasons, and you do not get to pick which ones you experience. Spring follows winter, summer follows spring, fall follows summer and winter follows fall. Selling has cycles, as well. In the spring we sow the seeds, in the summer those seeds germinate and take root, and we nourish, protect and defend the plants. In the fall, we harvest what we planted and take responsibility for our harvest. In the winter, we reflect, transform, and prepare for the next season.

S.O.S. tip: Get comfortable being uncomfortable with the constant movement and change. There is always good or a gift in every experience. Learn to notice, appreciate, and believe life is happening for you. Good times are followed by challenges; ride the waves. The more consistent we become with raising our selling standards and keeping in action, the less we will experience big swings in the waves because we have developed momentum. Nature loves speed!

The Law of Gestation. Everything takes time to manifest. You cannot put a tomato seed in the ground on day one and expect a live plant and twelve red, juicy tomatoes on day two. Everything in nature is both male and female. Creation requires both male and female energy. Ideas are spiritual seeds from the conscious mind (male energy), planted in the subconscious mind (female energy), and will move into form and physical results when the time is right. Know that they will. Your sales have gestation periods. Allow the seeds to take root and grow, then harvest at the appropriate time. Give them the attention and nourishment they need. Create value; it's the nourishment that brings a sale to life! Patience is key.

S.O.S. tip: Think and develop the mindset of a Gardner. Always be sowing, always be selling. Examine the soil, make space for the good you desire. Objections are nothing more than your clients' beliefs, attitudes and perceptions. Help the client to get in alignment with their desires. Eliminate the weeds. Nurture the new beliefs, hold the beliefs for the client until their belief gets affirmed. Have patience and allow Nature to do Her Part.

Below is my understanding of the seven Hermetic Principles from ancient Egypt and Greece for your reference, as they too, confirm principles of Universal law.

The Seven Hermetic Principles *"The Principles of Truth are Seven; he who knows these, understandingly, possesses the Magic Key before whose touch all the Doors of the Temple fly open." – The Kybalion*

1. **The Principle of Mentalism** – Mental transmutation gives you the ability to influence your reality. *"The ALL*

*is MIND; The ALL is in ALL; The Universe is Mental."-
The Kybalion*

2. **The Principle of Correspondence** – Your thoughts
   mirror your reality. Your outer world is a reflection of
   your inner world. Your dominating thoughts, the ones
   you give energy to are the ones that are meaningful. *"As
   above, so below; as below so above." – The Kybalion*

3. **The Principle of Vibration** – When we resonate with
   an emotion, we attract people who will bring more of it.
   Different manifestations of Matter, Energy, Mind, and
   Spirit result from various rates of vibration or frequency.
   The vibration of spirit is at an infinite rate of intensity
   and rapidity that it is practically at rest. At the other end
   of the scale, there are gross forms of matter whose
   vibrations are so low as they seem to be at rest. In
   between the two there are millions of frequencies.
   *"Nothing rests; everything moves; everything vibrates."
   – The Kyballion*

4. **The Principle of Polarity** – Everything has a sliding
   scale. What seems like opposites are actually varying
   degrees. *"Everything is Dual; everything has poles;
   everything has its pair of opposites; like and unlike are
   the same; opposites are identical in nature; but different
   in degree; extremes meet; all truths are but half-truths;
   all paradoxes may be reconciled." – The Kybalion*

5. **The Principle of Rhythm** – The pendulum of life is
   always swinging. Life's journey has peaks and valleys.
   The Hermetics's recognize that this pendulum of action
   and reaction, ebb and flow, applies to all the affairs of
   the Universe including the mental states of Man. They
   learn to use the principle instead of being used by it by
   polarizing themselves at the point they want to rest, and
   neutralize the rhythmic swing which would carry him to
   the other pole by the Law of Mental Neutralization.
   *"Everything flows, out and in; everything has tides; all
   things rise and fall; the pendulum-swing manifests in
   everything; the measure of the swing to the right is the*

measure of the swing to the left; rhythm compensates." –
The Kybalion

6. **The Principle of Cause and Effect** – Everything happens according to Law, nothing ever "merely happens." By self-mastery, raising awareness to a higher plane they become Causers instead of Effects. The Masters help play the game of life, instead of being played and moved about by others wills and environment. They use the principle instead of becoming its tool. They obey Causation of the higher planes, but help rule their own plane. *"Every Cause has its Effect; every Effect has its Cause; everything happens according to Law; Chance is but a name for law not recognized; there are many planes of causation, but nothing escapes the Law." – The Kybalion*

7. **The Principle of Gender** – Gender manifests in everything on the physical, mental and even the spiritual plane. No creation is possible without this principle. Everything and every person have both masculine and feminine energy. Masculine energy is goal oriented and action focused. Feminine energy is about taking a step back to reflect and re-evaluate; to look at the big picture and course correct. *"Gender is in everything; everything has its Masculine and Feminine Principles Gender; manifests on all planes." – The Kybalion*

Nature only punishes two things: Idleness and Vacuum.

Nature abhors a vacuum. The best way to avoid having a vacuum in your mind and having your thoughts drifting, going in all directions, is to fill your mind with a definite purpose. The definite purpose puts order in your mind to direct it toward the good you desire for yourself and others. Mind is movement, give order to the movement.

The second thing nature punishes is idleness. Napoleon Hill stated idleness of the mind is the workshop for the Devil. The best cure for idleness is to focus on your definite purpose. The Law of Use reminds us that what we do not use and invest, we will lose. Put your mind to use.

Spiritual Laws of Success Deepak Chopra distilled the essence of how Law, the divine vibration, applies to human behavior and our ability to deal with people to create harmony. Sales is a people business and our degree of emotional intelligence and awareness in how to deal with people certainly impacts our sales success. Let's review these laws.

The Law of Pure Potentiality. This law states that human beings can create anything, anytime, anywhere. We are a field of all possibilities. When we are silent to just *be*, we witness the intelligence within every living thing, and we practice non-judgement.

When you are fully present with curiosity, when you observe the beauty and intelligence in every human being you interact with, when you balance empathy with persuasion, you open the flow of your potential. When we are "being", in the present, we can respond. We can focus on creating value instead of competing with the IS-NESS of the NOW. The starting point is to be, observe, and discover the outcome desired by the client, AND *why* they want that outcome. The deeper you dig into the *why*, the more you tap into the vein of gold. Once you understand motive, apply your potential to creating value. The value creation process is the action, the doing that causes the receiving, the having, or the sale, to happen. The creation process invokes the head and the heart to create. When you activate your client's heart and hold belief in their ability to create possibilities, you serve them powerfully.

S.O.S tip: Be, do, and have, in that order. Be fully present and curious in your observation. Create value, then expect to receive. See the divinity in your client. Keep your empathy/ego balance in check. If you have what they need, do not let them off the hook. Acknowledge them. Be direct, honest, and loving. Build a bridge of belief and lead them across it to their promised land.

The Law of Karma. This law states to be conscious of your actions. Beware of conditioned reflexes that are constantly being triggered by people and circumstances into predictable behavior patterns. Reacting like this is making choices unconsciously. Be consciously aware that your future is generated by the choices you are making in every moment of your life. Choosing actions that bring happiness and success to others will bring happiness and success to you.

We've heard it before; actions speak louder than words. Your actions affect your attitude just as much as thoughts. In sales, people are always watching your actions, not necessarily believing your words. Customers also pick up on your vibration, just like a radio, so it's always good to do an attitude check before making a sales call. Why? Your attitude is your energy field, and customers can feel it. Put your self-interests aside and be mentally ready to serve. The Law of Karma works for you when your actions align with your words. When your primary focus and action is serving to bring others happiness and success, you can expect to receive the same.

S.O.S. tip: *Learn to pause and respond. Be present and bring your choices into your conscious awareness. Ask yourself two questions: What are the consequences of this choice? Will this choice bring happiness to me and those around me?*

Are my thoughts, feelings, and actions aligned in integrity? Remember the universe has a perfect accounting system. If you have a karmic debt to pay, learn from the experience, look for the seed of opportunity to tie the experience back to your dharma. Get back into the spirit of selling and realize it is part of your evolution.

The Law of Least Effort. Nature's intelligence functions with effortless ease for harmony. This law suggests that we accept people, situations, and events as they occur; that you take responsibility for your situation and all events seen as problems. Selling becomes effortless when we relinquish the need to defend our point of view, knowing that what is resisted will persist, and the use of force will negate. It's giving up attachment to the *how* and being open to receive from expected and unexpected sources. It's giving up control of another human being, knowing the only person we control is ourselves.

S.O.S. tip: *In sales, it is best not to get fixated on one deal or one customer; instead, be fixated on serving by increasing the quality and quantity of service. Remember tension tires, relaxation renews. Practice serenity. Accept people, situations, circumstances, and events as they are. Relinquish the need to defend or persuade others of your point of view. Take responsibility for your intentions and your situation. Trust the process to yield a harvest. Don't be a wave taking on the ocean. Instead, ride with the waves and keep sowing.*

The Law of Intention & Desire. This law states you must be clear with what you want, that clarity effects the desire. Desire is a triggering mechanism for action. And the action is where the receiving happens. When it comes to selling, start with an intention or a goal that is specific. When you are emotionally involved with it, via desire, you have the mechanics for fulfillment. Trust and accept when things do not go your way; there is a reason.

S.O.S tip: Attention energizes; Life and energy flow to where your attention goes. Only focus on what you want. Intention transforms energy and information. Intention in attention organizes and provides order. **An intention** *is something that is (1) framed in the positive, (2) focuses on what you want, (3) makes you responsible for the outcome, (4) inspires you to act, (5) is in the present tense, and (6) is bigger than any one goal.* **It empowers you. It defines the character traits you want to embody.** *Set an intention to show up to connect with people and share your gifts. Use it to get yourself in the Spirit of Selling!*

The Law of Giving and Receiving. This law states that you should give more of what you want to receive, that you should circulate wealth. Wealth comes on three planes: the spiritual, the intellectual, and material planes. For example, you can give care, affection, appreciation, empathy, and love, which are not material but very valuable. Giving and receiving is a circular process, like the blood in your body. Circulation is a continual flowing around, just like the solar system. We possess all sorts of riches that we can bestow upon one another. When you circulate your wealth in the sales process, with everyone you contact, your abundance will grow and expand.

S.O.S. tip: *Giving and Receiving are two sides of the same coin. The saying that it's better to give than receive is as silly as saying just exhale, don't inhale. You are worthy. Give abundantly and receive graciously. Keep circulating your gifts. The more circulation, the more life, love, and light you share; the more joy and fulfillment you experience. Spirit is circular movement with expansion – keep it going!*

The Law of Dharma. This law states that we have been manifested in the physical form for a purpose. Purpose is an emotion, a feeling we experience, the joy and fulfillment when we share it and serve those around us. It is our spiritual essence, the emotion that shows up when we show up.

S.O.S tip: Remember your WHY. When you are selling with purpose and passion to serve, you experience a life of fulfillment. In sales, when you tap into your purpose--your dharma—you experience your emotional heart power, your passions and compassion for others. Being in alignment with your purpose allows you to say yes to what is important and no to what is not. Alignment with purpose allows you to unleash and activate your true potential and inner power.

The starting point of all achievement is a definite purpose. – Napoleon Hill

The Law of Detachment. Allow yourself and others the freedom to be who they are. Embrace the uncertainty; allow solutions to spontaneously emerge. This is the path to freedom. Change is external; transitions are internal. Transitions begin by letting go. The neutral zone between old and new is an opportunity for creativity, renewal, and development. When we accept the uncertainty and stay in the present, we experience joy. Life is just an infinite game.

> *S.O.S. tip:* *Trade in your expectations for appreciations.* *Sales is an infinite game that changes often; Embrace uncertainty, embrace the gifts from every game, and experience freedom to create value continually, regardless of circumstance. Stay in the spirit of selling and enjoy the evolution.*

Biblical Laws. These two laws predicate the game rules for creating value in the marketplace. We don't have to like them, but we do want to understand them. Why? So, we don't get hurt by them and can use them to our advantage. They are the "Law of Use" and "The Law of Sowing and Reaping."

The Law of Use. This law states that what you do not use, you will lose. The best illustration of this is in the Parable of the Talents. The story goes that a master gave his three servants talents, a form of gold. The first servant got five, the second got two, and the third got one. The master instructed all three to *use* them, to see what good they could do. Upon his return, he asked for an update. The first servant replied, "I invested my five and now have ten." The second replied, "I invested my two and now have four." The third replied, "I wrapped mine up and hoarded it so no one could take it, and here it is." The master told the third servant, "Give your talent to the first."

You might say, "Well, that's not fair, everything should be even." But that's not how it works. There is no hoarding in nature. If you don't use what you have, you will lose it. If you do not put to work the muscles of your mind, you will lose them. If you do not put to work the muscles of your body to keep that six pack of abs, you will lose it. It is what it is, so accept it. Use the law to work for you, not against you. Always raise your standards to give greater quality and quantity of service. Make use of your assets. Make use of your time. Continually raise your standards and keep growing.

The Law of Sowing and Reaping. It states, "What you reap is what you have sown." If you want to know how to find the answer to your problem, look in the mirror. You are either working with this law or against it. There are seven key points to remember about this law:

(1) It's negative. If you sow bad seeds, you reap a bad harvest.

(2) It's positive. If you sow good seeds, you reap a good harvest.

(3) You do not reap what you sow, you always reap MORE.

(4) There are many ways to sow and reap, change your life, achieve financial independence, etc., not just one, so be creative, and use your imagination!

(5) Anyone can sow and reap; it's not limited to a select group of people.

(6) The whole truth is that sometimes you will lose. Just like in nature, a hailstorm can destroy a crop. When it happens, look for the good.

(7) If you do not sow, you do not reap.

Never come from a place of need when you are selling. When you come from a place of need, you lose. Always come from a place of abundance, that is where your power is.

Never beat yourself up. If you attempt to alter your behavior from a place of comparison, competition, and fear, you will use the will to beat yourself up.

Failure is feedback. If your harvest, your results are not what you expected, use the time to reflect and do some introspection on your behavior. Did I ask the best questions of my team and of the customers? Did I meet all the players? Did I uncover the need and the motives? Did I sell myself, the company, and the product? Did I ask for the commitment, or did I assume I had commitment? How much value did I create? What can I do to create more value? Who else can I serve? Did I use my time wisely? This requires THINKING. Remember, if we don't use our mental muscles, we lose them. Ask yourself, *"How can the law of sowing and reaping be leveraged to my advantage? How can I increase the quantity or quality of my service? How can I raise my standards? What can I create for the harmonious good for all concerned? Who else can use my services? How can I shorten my sales cycle? What process or system can I employ to gain more momentum? Do I need to sow more? Am I making proper use of my time? Am I using all my*

talents?" Know this, if you are giving and serving others with

use of your talents; the good must come back to you—it is law.

> *S.O.S tip: Always be sowing; Remember that you do not*
>
> *sow and reap in the same season. Refuse to become complacent.*
>
> *Complacency causes replacement.*

IV. Sell from the Inside Out.

Purpose, Motives, & Desire – The Law of Dharma

"Ego lives from the perception of 'What's in it for me?' Spirit comes from the perception of 'What is in me that is for you?'"

- Deepak Chopra

"There is one quality which one must possess to win, and that is definiteness of purpose, the knowledge of what one wants, and a burning desire to possess it." – Napoleon Hill

Have you ever wondered what it is that fuels the most successful people in the world? The people who are unstoppable? No matter what knocks them down, they just get right back up and keep going? I believe it is because they are in touch with and remember their purpose. Purpose fuels their desires, allows them to make decisions easily, puts order in their mind and gives them the experience of joy and fulfillment. They love what they are doing, and they know why they are doing it. Life is vivified and enlivened in these successful people because they are in alignment with their Dharma, their purpose, the WHY behind it all.

Would you like that for yourself? Wouldn't it be cool if everyone in the world was connected to their purpose, living a life of joy and fulfillment? Imagine if every day you woke up and were excited to be selling because you know you are in alignment with your purpose. You are doing what you love, working for fulfillment instead of duty! Sound too good to be true? I am here to tell you it's possible if you are willing to put some work and effort into understanding yourself and remembering why you are here.

The Law of Dharma is the belief and knowing that we all are here to serve humanity in some way with our unique talent and our unique way of expressing that talent. Dharma is a

Sanskrit word that means "purpose in life." Each and every one of us are unique expressions of the Divine, a divine center of operation that is born just right the first time. The Law of Dharma is your essence, your spirit, your purpose, your divine assignment. And when the need for what you do is matched up with your creative expression of that talent at an excellence level, affluence is created. It is important for every individual to focus on what you are here to give; this is the Law of Dharma.

Deepak Chopra explains there are three components to your Dharma. The first is to discover your true self and accept the idea that we are spiritual beings having a physical experience, and not the other way around. Think about that long and hard. Have you discovered the god or goddess within you that wants to be born, revealed, and to express your divinity? Your soul is your spirit, your essence, the life source within you. Your higher self, your soul, is your source of inner wisdom. When you connect with it, remember it; the conscious awareness of your timeless essence comes into the time-bound experience here on earth. It's a feeling of empowerment like no other.

The second component of Dharma is when we discover the unique expression of our talents. What is it that you can do better than anyone else on the planet? When you are doing that, you lose track of time. It takes you to the space of timeless awareness. The discovery of our unique talents allows us to enjoy ourselves and experience bliss. It allows us to create abundance in our life and in the lives of others. It is our birthright.

The third component of Dharma is your service to humanity, what you do with the second component to help and serve others. It's knowing how you are best suited to serve humanity. You find the answer by asking yourself: *How can I help?* instead of *What's in it for me?* The answer takes you to the domain of your spirit. Do what you love, have a passion for what you do. When your passion matches with the needs of humanity, you will experience wealth and abundance. Serve your fellow human beings with love. Love is resonance.

I did not recognize or remember what my purpose was until I was in my fifties. When I figured it out, it had a profound change on my life. What a blessing! I was involved in a mastermind group that was formed from a Matrix event I attended in Toronto, in July of 2019. Gavin, a member of my mastermind group, invited his brother Dave to be a guest speaker on our call. This guy Dave had an aura of confidence that I had never experienced before. He spoke with such clarity and conviction. Have you ever experienced a speaker that so captivates your curiosity and attention that you get out the pen and pray you can write fast enough to capture it all? That was me that day.

I remember calling my friend Liss afterwards to compare notes and make sure we got it all. I was totally blown away. He gave me distinctions about purpose, vision, and goals that I had never heard before. He said a purpose is constant, and it never changes. Purpose is not measurable because its infinite. He told us our purpose was all about spiritual growth. When you tap into it, you will be able to draw forth higher levels of energy and release that energy. He said purpose is based on our desire to serve. Our spirit, the life within, is always looking for expansion and greater expression. Wow. I was resonating with the message and I decided, that day, that I would figure out what my purpose was.

When you understand your purpose and align it with your career in sales, you will have the inspiration and desire to be in the spirit of selling on a daily basis! The easiest way to remember and unveil your purpose is to start asking yourself questions. What are you interested in? What are you passionate about? And what are your values? Why are these values, interests, and passions important to you? These are all clues.

Next, think about when you release the most energy. What naturally energizes you? What experiences cause you to grow? What experiences do you want to cause for yourself and others? When you show up in life, what are people getting access to? Ask your friends and family: "When I am around you what do you feel? What are you getting access to?" Think about the best environment you've been in, those times when you experienced expansive growth. Describe it.

What do you love? What fires you up? When you walk into a bookstore, what section do you normally gravitate to? What interests do you have? What are you doing, being, or having when time seems to stand still? What do you love to create? What values do you treasure the most? Did you choose those values, or did you accept them from someone else? If you allow yourself to freely choose your values today, what would you choose?

Who do you love to serve and how do you love to serve others? Who has been showing up automatically and naturally through your whole life?

Ask yourself, *Am I a teacher? A healer? A helper? A creator? An inventor? A collaborator? A leader? A voice? A musician? An entertainer? A detective? A servant for justice and harmony? An artist? A caregiver?*

Another clue is to ask yourself: *What was I criticized for as a child?* As an example, if you are a teacher or leader, perhaps you were criticized for being bossy. You may have been criticized because people wanted you to conform, but you were expressing and trying out your individualized unique talents. When you recognize your purpose, you honor yourself – and consciously bring that essence to your work.

Purpose is often confused with roles. Roles are not your purpose; roles are multiple ways you can live out your purpose. I can think of multiple roles I've had over the first fifty years of my life—different ways to live my purpose. Cheerleader, student, Drill team, Best Friend, Football Mom, Waitress, Sister, Sales representative, Sales Manager, Sales Director, Mother, CCD teacher, Wife, Daughter, Aunt, Coach, Author, Speaker etc. Think of roles as different coats your try on for greater expansion and expression of your purpose during different stages of your life.

Without purpose, you drift. Look at what happens with New Year's resolutions. By March, most of us have retreated to the comfort zone of habitual behavior. Have you ever had a sales year when you started to drift? Perhaps you got off to a slow start or felt like you were just going through the motions. Chances are you were distracted or bored or viewing your position from duty instead of joy and expression. Or the "escape clause" took over and you decided to settle.

If you are not familiar with the escape clause, it sounds like this: "I'm going to do it as soon as…" Fill in the blank. You make decisions based on what you have versus what you want and love. It's a common sales objection. We let an idea die because we don't know *HOW* to do it. We cope and cooperate and tell ourselves we should be happy with what we have. Where's the inspiration in that? They say "rationalizing" is the process we use to ration lies to ourselves. Many of our clients have let their dreams die. They are settling for things they do not want. And therein lies the opportunity for a sale. We serve others when we help them separate lies from truth. The more we understand the importance of purpose, for ourselves and the others we serve, the more excellence we bring into the quality of our service.

So, how do you stop yourself or others from drifting or settling? Activate desire. Desire is a want that you emotionalize and impress on your subconscious mind. When desire is impressed, your vibration or feeling is altered, and you are driven to act and behave differently. Desire comes alive when we are in alignment with the Law of Dharma. When we know what we want and WHY. A car cannot run on an empty tank of gas, nor can goals become reality without the proper fuel. Passion is the fuel for the heart's desire, and when you can recognize what fuels you and what fuels the passion in your clients, selling will become effortless. All sales are made based upon desire; the benefit is what sells, not the feature. Desire and Dharma bring us into a high-speed vibration of love and resonance.

Is there a difference between purpose and work? Indeed! Purpose never changes, although the forms to express the spirit's essence may change. Think of your purpose as the center of your divinity, the Sun in your "soul" system. You are a soul with a mind, living in a physical body. You operate on three planes simultaneously. Your job may or may not be a direct link to your essence, the spirit of you. Often people find themselves in a job out of duty instead of purpose. Work was designed for you, so you can express your talents. Do what you love. Ask yourself, "What is my purpose?" and start looking for the answer. Seek to remember.

I did the work and found my purpose—what a blessing, what an energy boost to my life. I can now make decisions easily when I know that decision is aligned with my purpose. But I was curious, why did it take me over fifty years to figure this out? The answer is programming and conditioning. There is a phenomenal book, *The Mastery of Self* by Don Miguel Ruiz Jr., that I recommend to all my clients. In it, he describes that we each live in our own personal dream, and that all of our sufferings occur when we forget we are the architects of our own reality.

My take on it is this? There are only three things in life that hold us back or cause struggle; they are our beliefs, our perceptions, and our attitudes. At birth, the soul arrives on the planet knowing what its purpose is. Each soul, upon arrival into physical form, is endowed with an intellect and a physical body. The greatest gifts bestowed on us from our creator are the marvelous mind, and time. Those who learn how to utilize and invest those gifts enjoy great happiness.

The mind and our ability to speak words are what separates us from the animal kingdom. Think of the mind as a new personal computer. The mind has two components or capabilities; one capability is deductive programming, meaning it is indifferent and will accept whatever program it is given. The second capability is a latent capability. It provides the soul with the capability to create its own environment and the free will to create thought, and accept or reject thoughts; this choice software is our personal power, our inductive reasoning. I say "latent" to point out that this secondary software program has a gestation period of six to eleven years before it is fully functional.

So, how do we get by in those first six years? We become programmed and conditioned based upon our environment and genetics. We were created by a union of Mom's egg with Dad's sperm. All the programming and conditioning of our genetics is passed on to us in our cells. The environment we grow up in, everything we see, hear, feel, or touch from our surroundings in those initial six years impacts our programing. We learn to accept the beliefs of our parents, family, friends, and teachers.

We have no ability to reject what we are exposed to until our choice software becomes active, at around age six. This is when we spit out the peas, start saying no, and start asking, "Why?" It's a time to be celebrated—our inductive reasoning has arrived! But all too often, instead of a celebration, we receive fear-based conditioning to get us to conform. In fact, most of our conditioning is fear based. Fear is a low-level vibration that holds us back. To maintain control, so we would behave appropriately, our parents tried their best to persuade us. "Johnny, if you eat your dinner, we will go out for ice cream." When that didn't work, they resorted to fear-based tactics; if this, then that. And that's how we learn and experience that love is conditional. It's the fear of loss of love that causes the child to seek approval, to conform, and to compete for attention. That's when we start to forget our purpose; that's when we put on the mask; we forget how to just be ourselves, and the conditioning takes our power away.

We learn our name through repetition. We develop our self-image based upon how our family, friends, and those in our environment perceive us. Maxwell Maltz tells us our self-image is not who we think we are, or who others think we are, but it is who we think others think we are. It comes from conditioning versus choice. We never learn to ask ourselves questions. Why do I believe that? Is it really true? Does this belief serve me, or empower me? If not, what belief would empower me and serve me? Why am I holding onto this belief so tightly? What am I gaining from this belief? What is it costing me? If I changed that belief, what could I gain? What would I lose with the new belief?

Remember this: those who love you did their best. They shared their software with you, but they could only give you what they had. If they had any limiting beliefs, you most likely accepted them. It wasn't your fault, but now that your awareness has expanded, it is your responsibility to take your power back, to choose your beliefs, perceptions, and attitudes. And remember this: have some empathy. Everyone around you has been programmed, hypnotized, and most likely has forgotten their purpose.

Jesus was a teacher who taught this form of radical conscious awareness, and he practiced it. He was the greatest salesman. He saw the divinity in everyone around Him, be it the leper, the tax collector, the Apostles, the disciples, or the Pharisees. He saw through the programming; he saw the good within everyone. He had empathy. It is the good, the talent, the unique gift that each one of us has that is looking to be unleashed for greater expression and expansion. It's the conditioning that keeps people in a hypnotic state. Jesus spoke from His Higher Self to the Higher Self of others, calling everyone to draw the God or Goddess from within, to unfold, and become the very best version of themselves. When we get in the spirit of selling, we want to do the same: see through the hypnosis; see the divinity in every individual.

The other area to examine when we speak about forgetting our purpose is awareness, based upon the emotional hierarchy of human needs, also known as motives. Napoleon Hill trained many salespeople, and he made a profound statement in his speech on Definiteness of Purpose. He said that a sales professional has no right to ask anyone to do anything at any time without giving that person an adequate motive. A motive is the emotional reason a person takes action. Knowing the motive in sales is important for persuasion.

Motives allow you to identify and evoke your client's emotions to take action. Hill outlined nine basic motives. Motives for human behavior are not typically found in the sales textbooks, but they are in the psychology books. Seven of the ten motives are positive, three are negative. They are:

Desire for Self-preservation/safety;

Desire for Material gain;

The emotion of Love;

The emotion of Sex;

Desire for freedom of body and mind;

Desire for Recognition and Self-expression;

Desire for Life after death/Self-actualization;

The emotion of Fear;

The emotion of Anger

The emotion of Hate/Revenge.

There are six basic fears, they are: the fear of poverty, the fear of ill health, the fear of criticism, the fear of loss of love, the fear of old age, and the fear of death. Buyers' motives tell us the WHY behind what they are looking to accomplish, fix, or avoid. You always want to know what the client wants, and why, before you attempt to sell anything. No want, no sale. People buy ideas and benefits, not merchandise. People buy based on their emotions and justify their emotions with logic. When you study the motives, study yourself. What are your motives? Recognize the opportunity that lies within understanding yourself. The more you understand yourself, the more you will understand your clients.

When we live and sell from the space of our divine purpose, we discover our Higher Self and our divinity. When we express our unique talents in in our unique way, we allow ourselves to be, do, and have what we love. We lose track of time. We become fully present where our true power lies. When we give that same gift to our clients, we gain their cooperation, trust, and free them to experience their own wants, desires, and dreams.

Courage, competence, and confidence instantly appear, and we take off our mask and get comfortable just being ourselves. It feels amazing. We experience authenticity. This is when the magic happens. For any of you that practice yoga, remember the word *Namaste*. It means the light in me recognizes the light in you.

You are important. You have important work to do, and you were sent here for a reason. You came through your parents, not to them, to express and expand your spirit, your essence, and to share it with others on this planet. You are here to take your place in the universe, and your place can only be filled by you. You are a child of the universe. There is no one with your exact talent or gift, no one with your unique way of expressing that gift. You are a light that the world needs to see. The more you study yourself, the more likely you will remember why you are here.

I have led many leadership workshops on finding purpose, and it is paradoxical, how many people in attendance will say *I don't know what my purpose is*. It's a paradox because our purpose often goes unnoticed as a natural part of our being, how we typically show up. It is so natural for us that we think everyone has what we have, and we fail to see how we are unique and divine. So, we miss seeing the divinity in everyone that surrounds us.

What about you? Is your purpose lying dormant, or is it hidden from you? How often do you see and recognize the divinity that surrounds you? What would it be like if you were living from the heart space of living out of your Dharma, recognizing you have a gift, working to develop it, and perfecting that gift to be the best possible version of yourself? What might that do for your sales results? Know this: when you turn away from your spirit, your true essence, life, and selling, become stressful. When you are in alignment with your purpose,

selling is effortless. Get into the spirit of it!

Chapter V –Where your Attention Goes, the Energy Flows!

"The Law of Vibration" and the "Law of Intention and Desire"

"You become what you think about most of the time and that's the strangest secret." – Earl Nightingale

"Setting goals is the first step of turning the invisible to the visible." – Tony Robbins

"You want to set a goal that is big enough that in the process of achieving it you become someone worth becoming." – Jim Rohn

"It's not Hocus Pocus, it's your focus." – Mary Morrisey

Your mind can create anything you desire. Your mind is an instrument that creates by vibration. The Law of Vibration states everything is always moving. Your mind is movement. You are a creator by design, you can shape energy. The question is are you consciously choosing what you create for yourself in your world? Do you know how to deliberately operate the instrument of your mind? Do you realize you create your desires daily, either by default or design? Hopefully I have your attention.

Mark McCormack, in his book, *What They Don't Teach You at Harvard Business School*, tells of a study conducted between 1979 and 1989 with graduates of the MBA program at Harvard. Eighty-four percent of the graduates had no specific goals other than graduating and enjoying their summer. Thirteen percent of the graduates had meaningful worthy goals, but they were not written down. Three percent of the graduates had written worthy goals and plans.

Ten years later, the thirteen percent who had formed the habit of setting goals earned twice as much as the eighty-four percent who did not set goals. The three percent who had formed the habit of setting goals and writing them down earned, on average, ten times as much than the other ninety-seven percent! Why do you suppose that is? They set goals. They had declared the direction they would move in. They set an intention and pursued their desires. Goals give order to the movement.

Selling is about creating value for customers, persuading clients to move in a direction toward their promised land. Selling is directing movement. Think of yourself in the role of a value creator because that is what the true sales pros are. Sales Goals force us to think and to utilize our most valuable asset, the mind, and help us learn and understand the laws and rules of the game to create, how to give order and direction to the movement.

There are never any mistakes in life, only lessons. When we think, we invoke the imagination. It's the workshop of the mind where the blueprints and plans are drawn. All thoughts are on a frequency. We alter our vibration and our awareness, based upon our thoughts and our thoughts activate the law of perpetual transmutation. The process of being a goal achiever is the process of creation, moving to different frequencies. The verb, think, according to the dictionary means, "to form in the mind, conceive, imagine, to determine by reflection; to formulate a way through difficulty; or to get rid of." Whatever you conceive, believe, desire, and feel is realized in your experience. A goal achiever knows that his mind creates his world.

This chapter is so fun to write because understanding the power behind writing and achieving goals is the way to take your power back. There is only one mental disease -unawareness. The more conscious awareness increases, the less ignorance exists. Setting goals, moving towards them, is the path for increased awareness. Understanding this is your ticket to freedom. Happiness, joy, adventure, bliss, and fulfillment rise as your awareness rises.

Most schools don't offer a course in goal achievement. The goal setting process is one of the most misunderstood concepts of human behavior. If goal setting and achievement were truly understood, everyone would be engaged in the behavior. If sales organizations knew what their top performers were doing—those who consistently meet and exceed sales targets, they would train the rest of the team to apply those same principles. But many achievers are unconsciously competent. That is, they're unaware of why they're winning. I know I was. And those who do not consistently achieve their goals lack understanding of the principle behind setting them or do not set the right type of goal.

Most sales trainings up to this point, have focused on the mechanics of selling instead of the principles behind the winning behavior. If you get nothing else from this book, recognize there is a principle behind goal setting, and power behind aiming for something specific. It's controlled attention in action. Controlled attention has intensity, increases amplitude of vibration, and releases power. It works like a flashlight or magnifying glass – whatever you focus on grows!

Many people view goals as a "to do" or "should do" list. They set goals from a logical place. They use their conscious mind and aim at something they've already done, or at something they think they can do. Corporations often set revenue targets based on what they've done in the past. They base revenue predictions on new product introductions and infrastructure changes. Very few companies allow themselves to set a Big Hairy Audacious Goal—something they would love; despite the fact they do not know HOW they will get there. If they can't explain the HOW, typically they dismiss the idea. What a shame – it's the ignorance that holds them back.

When you ask successful people what they think about most of the time, the answer is *what they want* and *what action they can take to get it*. Successful people are masters at focusing their attention subjectively. That means from within. They deliberately choose their preoccupations.

In contrast, unsuccessful people are thinking about *what they do not want*—too many bills, not enough money, the competitor, what if they say no, or can they afford it? They suffer from the distraction of shiny objects. Their attention is directed objectively to external impressions. It's like turning on a water hose without a human hand to direct the water. The mind is going in all kinds of directions.

All success, progress, and fulfillment of desire is based in direct proportion with the ability to direct and control your attention. Earl Nightingale called this truth "The Strangest Secret." Your attention is always on, just like the water in the hose, the question is are you always on, directing its focus?

Sales people are paid to achieve and exceed their goals. The company's annual sales target is the revenue the company needs to cover expenses and generate a profit. Cash flow is the critical oxygen that circulates within an organization to keep it alive. Without sales, the organization will die. Goal setting is commonplace to sales organizations, but goal achievement is variable. Most commercial organizations hire salespeople and provide them with a goal, or a quota: *Here's our revenue target!*

A salesperson's compensation revolves around this goal. Sales results are monitored on a scorecard. You are either on target, exceeding target, or below the target, at any point during the year. Sales performance and scores are like a football game with four quarters. The score tells you where you are and where you need to go to win the game. There are no second chances or replays. You have four quarters to get the job done. The objective of the game is mastery of yourself and your attention. The most efficient and effective use of time and skill wins.

Total compensation packages for salespeople can vary. Most of them employ external drivers for motivation. But maybe there's a better recipe, and maybe it's internal: awareness of the subconscious mind and how to use it to achieve goals. Goal setters work with the conscious logical mind, the servant. The conscious mind is where the ego resides, and recollection of what has been done before, all the limiting beliefs. Goal achievers work with and lean into the subconscious mind, the master. They use subjective control of their attention. Goal achievers do the illogical. If you understand the principles that guide the subconscious mind, goal achievement becomes an effortless process. It takes some work to build the muscle, apply the faith, but the payoff is increased conscious awareness, the true prize.

If we are going to be in the Spirit of Selling, understanding the secret to goal achievement is paramount. The more you understand the power of the process—what goal setting really is and what causes people to achieve their goals—the more enthusiasm you will have towards setting Big Hairy Audacious Goals! Everything in life has two parts, the essential and the incidental, the cause and the effect. We have access to untapped potential, but sometimes we lean into mechanics for support when, instead, we should be thinking about the principle of creation. The cause of goal achievement is the impression and concentration of thought on the formless substance from which all things are made. The key word is concentration and concentration is an effect from focused attention. The power and the potential in every organization is in the human mind capital and the human heart power. Organizations that know WHY they are in business and have an inspired workforce will always soar. Simon Sinek describes this scenario as playing the infinite game utilizing the power of the human heart in his book *"Start with Why."*

What I am about to share with you is my interpretation of the metaphysics behind goal achievement. Let's apply it to meeting and achieving sales. I'll break it down into essential steps. There is a governing principle, or law, that lives in harmony with each step. If you accept these new ideas and apply them, you will become courageous and confident in your ability to create goals and achieve them. If you lead others in your organization to adopt and apply these ideas, your organization will experience lasting abundance.

You are a spiritual being who has an intellect and lives in a physical body. You live in an ocean of motion. You can direct the Law of Perpetual Transmutation with your controlled attention. Everything is moving. Your mind is movement.

Let me explain. When babies are born, it takes time for them to maneuver their bodies, to learn how to walk and talk. It's because the spirit and essence of the soul arrives in a physical body and learns by observation. A baby looks around and sees all these giant figures. A baby looks at his hand and wonders, what is this? They bite their own finger and realize it belongs to them. They feel hunger and through Mom's repetition of "Open wide Johnny." and seeing her open her mouth to put food in, Johnny learns to open his mouth to eat. We learned to survive by observation. The problem is once we developed our inductive reasoning, somewhere between three and six years of age, we developed a habit of playing Monkey see, Monkey do, and kept playing that game. Grade school doesn't say, "Don't forget Johnny, you were born in the image of your creator and you can create your world. You can choose to accept, reject, neglect, originate any idea." Instead, Johnny hears, "Get with us here in reality. Stay within the lines. Where did you get that idea? – how are you going to do that?" Johnny doesn't know HOW, but up until this point, he never worried about HOW, he just focused on what he wanted. Because he wants approval and wants to please to fit in, to be recognized and respected, and he doesn't know HOW, he starts letting go of that dream and the imagination muscle atrophies. He starts to accept the masses consciousness to settle.

The body is the instrument for the mind. You are not your body. Einstein's brain is preserved in New Jersey, but he isn't there. The soul has left his body and organs. Bodies deteriorate in caskets and turn to dust when a person dies. The soul moves on because everything in the universe is always moving. Nothing is created or destroyed. The ocean is always moving. So is the earth, the moon, and the stars, and so are you. This is the Law of Vibration.

Thought is movement.

When you are with a client, are you and your attention staying with them in the present, in the room, or is your thought taking you and your attention out of the room worrying about what to say next, or when you need to pick up your child or what you are going to tell your boss? Yes, your body is there but where is your attention focused? Did you travel and leave the conversation for a while? If so, that's why you missed a few things that could have helped you create more value. Worse yet, did your client travel and leave the conversation during your meeting? Did you keep their attention or did they drift? See what I mean about thought is movement?

Go to your imagination with me and picture yourself observing a marina next to the ocean. Let's allow ourselves to accept the idea that a soul or spirit lives in each boat, floating in this ocean of movement we call the universe. Pretend the boat is the soul's physical body, a vessel to use for the journey on earth. Each boat has a fishing net attached to it. That fishing net can catch thoughts, just like fish, some are positive, some are negative. Where the soul focuses its attention is the direction the soul moves in. Let's say the attention is the sail of the boat, your goal. There are many boats in the ocean, and they come in various shapes and sizes. As you observe the environment, you notice some boats are idle, not sure where to go. The ignition and motor are turned on, the spirits in them are breathing, and you watch them get tossed wherever the wind blows. They drift, and quite often, they get caught up in the rocks. These idle boats have spirit in them, but no awareness of how to steer the boat. You hear these idle boats in the marina. They talk with one another, about the safety and benefit of staying close to the shore, about avoiding risk. The sails are not set, the boats are rocking going whether the wind blows.

You look out on the ocean and observe other boats headed away from the marina. The souls in these boats sense the urge to explore and have an adventure. But some of those souls venture out and then return back to the dock after they get out a few miles. They rationalize staying put. Translated, they "ration lies" to themselves. They use the escape clause, "I will as soon as….fill in the blank." The dream of the soul dies, and the boat of that soul never leaves the dock. Yet the others in that group feel compelled to act on that desire and intention for adventure. They utilize curiosity to study the boat and learn how to set a sail, how you can manipulate a sail to go in the direction you want to go, regardless of the wind. They take it for a test drive, and are willing to sacrifice whatever it takes to pursue the dream. Their curiosity and desire cause their awareness to expand, and they discover the steering wheel exists and how to use it. They set their sails toward a destination; they press on and take off in a specific direction, sailing across the expanse of the ocean!

What's the difference? What do those folks enamored with a destination know? What information do they possess that the masses in the marina are ignorant to? These winners understand they are creators capable of designing their life by controlling their attention. They understand all current results are the result of the frequency they are operating from; that the frequency is their level of awareness. If they want something different, something more, they will need to travel to that new frequency destination. They grab the steering wheel and listen to their heart. They draw up a blueprint and vision for the direction they want to move in. They know that the moment they decide to chart a new course, and refuse to stay where they are, the declaration of purpose with an obsessional desire alters the vibration frequency. And they learn to trust their emotional guidance system. These individuals possess courage and confidence, and they accept full responsibility to control their thoughts and attention, to create their experiences, and be the cause of their own lives. And the more they do that, the more their confidence and faith in themselves soar.

These individuals have appreciation of their greatest asset, their mind. These individuals are in harmony with the spiritual law of intention and desire. They attract all that is required via the universal law of vibration! They are the goal achievers who know, "We become what we think about." Goal achievers think into results. Which boat do you want to be in?

The book, *Think and Grow Rich,* by Napoleon Hill wrote the recipe to achieve your goal in six steps. Here is my understanding:

FIRST: You must fix in your mind exactly what you want. Ask yourself these questions, "Where am I now and where do I want to be? If I could have absolutely anything that I want, what would I love?" DESIRE, is the voice of your soul, awareness of an emotionalized WANT. Your desire is unique to you. Everything you want is already here. The question is are you willing to do what it takes to reveal it? Ask yourself, "Why do I want it?" Describe it in detail – the Universe loves

CLARITY. Be definite. SMART goals are specific and measurable. If your desire is vague, your results will be vague.

The best example and evidence of a vague goal from my experience was my first marriage. I fell in love with the idea of getting married by the time I was thirty. I wanted two kids, preferably one boy and one girl. I met my first husband at the gym. His goals were the same as mine. We had a ton of things in common. Whatever you put out to the universe you get back. The law of attraction brought us together. We both were crystal clear that we wanted a marriage and a family in our thirties; we wanted kids. But we never talked about what we wanted in the marriage. We never talked about what we wanted from each other, while we were parenting, and afterward. Our ideas were different, not fused. So, the marriage intimacy part had no life in it. I was caught up in duty but not experiencing joy and fulfillment in the relationship. We had conditional love instead of unconditional love.

When I was forty, I found unconditional love. I decided to use my free will and choose love over duty. I blew up my first marriage. I was condemned and criticized, but I gained an amazing amount of wisdom from my failure. I didn't understand at the time how important the clarity piece was for the marriage. I did realize I caused my life, that I was responsible for the mess. I got exactly what I asked for and nothing more. There are no mistakes in life, only lessons.

SECOND: Determine exactly what you intend to give or give up in return for the goal you desire. Feel worthy of receiving it. There is no such thing as "something for nothing." Sacrifice is making space by giving up something of a lower nature for one of a higher nature. This is a super important point to remember while selling. Every decision means a sacrifice. If your customers are stalling or saying no to you, they haven't made a decision to leave port and make a sacrifice to change, give something old up for something new.

Take action and pay it forward. You can't get heat from a fire without putting the logs in first. Earning more commission might mean selling higher ticket items instead of lower ticket ones. It might mean giving up a bad habit and replacing it with one that empowers you, and enhances your skill. It may mean getting up one hour earlier each day to increase your productivity or delegating more of your duties or responsibilities to others who can support you and gain their self-confidence and self-reliance from your gift. Remember giver's gain. The more you give, the more you feel fulfilled, and the more worthy you will feel. You can always get better and as you increase the value you provide others, the value of you is worth more. As you focus on the good you see in others, the more self-worth you will see in you.

THIRD: Establish a definite date when you intend to possess what you want and give thanks. "Someday" is not definite, its day dreaming. We do not know the exact gestation of an idea but the date creates a sense of urgency. If you set a financial sales goal for the year, then the date is on or before December 31st.

FOURTH: Create a definite plan with milestones. Break the goals down into Months, weeks and days. Get clear on the daily goal – the present is where your power is. All we have is NOW. Whether you are ready or not, begin at once to put the plan into massive action.

FIFTH: Write out the goal, name the time limit for its acquisition, what you intend to give or give up for what you will receive. Write out your plan. The writing causes thinking. We think in pictures. The picture is the mold for you to shape the power. The more you hold it still with controlled attention, the sooner it will come into physical form. The pictures cause feeling, feeling causes action. Your feeling is the tuning dial for your mind that shifts you onto a different vibration frequency. Assume the wish is fulfilled and FEEL it. Use your emotional guidance system. Assumption is the speed of light that Einstein referred to in e=mc2. It throws you into warp speed like on Star Trek to "There" which is a place. It's the magic that activates the law of perpetual transmutation. If you do not impress the want with the feeling, you are not going to activate gestation and move to the new frequency; you will just be wishing and day dreaming.

SIXTH: Make a committed DECISION, to cut the cord, burn the bridges, leave the marina, and turn away from the shore and toward the ocean, move toward your goal, —making this committed decision and declaration immediately alters one's VIBRATION; Committed does not mean when it's convenient, it means accept no excuses, only results. Refuse to stay where you are on the old frequency. No more escape hatches such as, "I will as soon as..." Have courage and confidence in yourself and your power. Read your written goal twice daily after rising and before retiring at night.

Understand at first you will be uncomfortable, perhaps even fearful, because your body does not have cells of recognition of the new you operating at the new frequency. This is where persistence and applied faith comes in. You must believe it to receive it. The Nazorean two thousand years ago stated it many times in many ways. *"As you believe, so shall it be done to you."* Expectancy is the Law of Attraction, the secondary Law to the Law of Vibration. Grow your beliefs to meet your new desires so they fuse, that creates the magnetism power to bring you everything you need.

The easiest road to build belief is auto-suggestion and writing out the goal. Eventually you will believe. Affirming the goal out loud, re-writing the goal in the present twice a day, seeing the goal, acting as if the wish is fulfilled and feeling it helps you reinforce the new neural pathway. The more you write the goal out and say the affirmations, the more cells of recognition you are making to pull that picture front and center with your attention. Being YOU in the vision is different from watching YOU in the vision. When you watch yourself, you are longing; when you are being the new you and acting as if, you are now on the frequency. The plans are flexible for the journey ahead. Remember the order: be, do, have.

SEVENTH: Finally, and most IMPORTANT, ask the essential for help; have humility, and remember your role is to co-create with the power by directing your attention with your thoughts. Your goal card is your Prayer. You are the instrument that directs the power. The Power does the work. Energy and information exist everywhere in nature, and the nature of the universe is "order" (law) and "movement" (mind). The more "ordered" the movement becomes, the greater the manifestation power. Goal achievement is the process of bringing the unmanifest or invisible into the visible. The principle behind the concept of goal achievement is to understand what influences energy movement and manifestation. When you understand, you will realize that things are not impossible, but you are "I AM possible." You never have to settle or stay where you are. A goal is the direction you move in to "BECOME" and create the best version of yourself. The "BE" happens first. It is the cause; the deed or result comes second; it is the effect. You are the cause; the sale is the effect.

Human beings are a privileged species in the scheme of nature, in that we have "self-consciousness." Our nervous system can become aware of energy and information that gives rise to our physical body. We experience the energy field subjectively in our thoughts, feelings, desires, beliefs, creative faculties, and instincts. Think of yourself as a wave in a big ocean, or a radio frequency, or a localized disturbance in a larger quantum field. Your consciousness is infinitely flexible. All that is required to alter consciousness is a desire to BE and a decision to define or declare "I AM." The tools we use to change energy and information are two qualities in our consciousness: attention and intention.

Whatever we give attention to grows, becomes energized. Energy is always running to and through us. Think of attention as one's ability to cause magic. Attention is like having a magic flashlight; you choose where to aim it and what to focus on; whatever is focused on through the flash light or one's attention, will grow.

Intention, the second quality of consciousness, triggers "transformation" by its infinite organizing power, which means the power to organize an infinity of time-space events, all at the same time. Remember, the more orderly and organized the movement, the more potent and powerful that energy becomes.

When I was a little girl, there was a TV show called Bewitched. Samantha could simply wiggle her nose to put things back in order. Your intent is that bewitching power within. Intent has infinite flexibility. If the intent is for the harmonious good of all concerned, universal intelligence will always give you the ability to bring forth the unmanifest to the manifest.

Intention has no attachment; it is only concerned with the end result of the intention. This is important. Remember, the "how" is none of your business. The dictionary defines intention as the aim to create, or a plan. Intention is analogous to an investment; intention is a commitment to carry out an action or actions for the future. It's your God-given creative ability. To give something for the future is letting go of the brakes. It's living and being inspired by the confidence of a bright future.

Desire acts like a fuel distributor and fuel injection system for your boat. Think of desire as the release mechanism that opens up to allow energy to go and flow more freely. We always release energy. You intensify and develop an obsessional desire by controlled attention. Desire makes energy flow faster and more powerfully. Desire has urgency, not hurry, and there is a difference. Hurry is afraid, but urgency has courage and confidence. Urgency becomes effortless by positive assumption. Our actions and behavior reflect our desire level. When desire has urgency, the energy increases the vibration that causes the change in frequency and attracts everything you need for the new aim. Desire is based on what you would love, the idea that resonates with you. Desire mixed with urgency causes manifestation by law.

When you are not inspired or moving forward, vibration declines and causes disintegration. Complacency causes replacement. If you want a good example of what complacency looks like in salespeople, watch the movie *Glengarry Glen Ross*. Make sure you don't see yourself as one of the three real estate agents sitting at their desks, simply breathing, about to be replaced, full of excuses, and expecting someone to hand them the leads!

You were born to take risks. Risk-taking is how you grow and become more. It is how you gain more awareness, and awareness is the name of the game in life. How far can you expand your awareness before your time here on earth is up?

Those who are risk adverse, those who play it safe, give their power away. If that's you, ask yourself, why? You never did that when you were a kid. Babies are not afraid to learn how to walk. Kids persist to figure out how to ride a bike. Kids learn to hit a baseball with a bat through persistence. Teenagers learn how to drive a car to gain some freedom. They take a risk in asking someone to go out on their first date, so they can experience a first kiss.

These examples are all learner goals, inspirations with intention and desire. Every accomplishment has given you more self-confidence and self-esteem. Creation breeds self-confidence, self-reliance, and self-esteem. The question you want to ask yourself honestly is, "Do I really think I know everything? What don't I know? What more can I learn? What am I creating today? More of the same or something new? Am I stretching myself? Or Am I settling and docking myself in the marina? If so, why? What do I need to BELIEVE to allow myself to be empowered to go after those big hairy audacious goals?"

In 2019 we witnessed the legend Tiger Woods win the Masters for the fifth time. Today, as I write this book, Tom Brady appeared in his tenth Superbowl and won his first NFC Superbowl Championship. I am truly fascinated by Tiger and Tom, by their demonstration of mastery of self, the mastery of attention with intention. Tiger Woods and Tom Brady represent two examples of people who display competence in using their mind for continual goal achievement. I believe Tiger and Tom are experiencing life as an infinite adventure, and I assume they know that they cause life for themselves, that they do it by design. They are the stars of their individual movies. They do not compete; they continuously create.

That's what goal achievement is all about—a new direction for more BE, a direction for creating new experiences and growth for yourself and others. Goal achievement is an act of stewardship. When you use your talents to become more, to give more, you realize it is not about you; it is for something bigger than yourself. Intent, the transformation power, is to leave the place better than you found it for those who come behind you, and the reward is fulfillment. Why? You are not thinking about you; you are focused on serving others. When you observe successful salespeople, you can see and feel their joy and fulfillment in the moment because they are doing what they love to do, and they love to serve others.

So how can we, who choose the profession of selling for a lifetime, experience fulfillment? How do we experience timeless success? Remember you are a creator. You co-create with the power daily; you are the instrument that directs the power. Your thoughts and feelings are analogous to the set of the sail. Selling is doing something for people with Universal Power. Source energy is the essential, and you are the incidental, the distribution center for good. Every transformation begets more conscious awareness. It's wisdom. It's gold! I like to think of it as an infinite game. How far can I go? How much awareness can I gain while on this journey through life?

Before you pursue your goal, it is important to know where you are. Knowing where you are is the process of self-evaluation. If you want to jump on a plane to visit Japan, you need to know what airport you will be flying out of right?! The same principle applies to goal achievement. The practice of regular self-examination is paramount to our success in goal achievement. If we want to be good conduits for the power within, to have the one and only source flow through us, at a high speed of vibration, and with power, we want to keep our circuitry clean and clear of blockages. The greater the circulation and movement of energy for the good of all concerned, the more that energy will come back, just like the waves in the ocean.

On my website, www.thespiritofselling.com, you will find self-analysis tools that will engage you in introspection of yourself, your current level of consciousness, and your current personal standards. Stop right now, download the document and take 30 minutes to answer the questions honestly.

Champions put the work in up front. They act. Will you? Trust me, this is life changing. Socrates said, *"The unexamined life is not fit for human living."* You cannot be two selves at the same time standing with one foot in and one foot out. You must decide which person you want to be and align the life-giving forces of your being with that side. If you don't, you will suffer from ambivalence and indecision. You will need to let the old self go and make room for the new.

Jesus said, *"If therefore thine eye be single [if your consciousness be pure and one-pointed], thy body shall be full of light."* The Chinese have a precept that says, *"Not to correct our faults is to commit new ones."*

So now that you understand the principles behind goal setting and achievement, what goal will inspire you to create something new for yourself or others? What goal will take you towards a quantum leap in your awareness? Set a direction forward into the sea of Conscious Awareness. Choose to go for what you love and develop the discipline to direct your attention with intention. The day you achieve mastery of controlling your attention in your subjective mind, you will become the master of your fate.

"My mind is a center of Divine Operation. The divine operation is always for expansion and fuller expression, and this means the production of something beyond what has gone before, something entirely new, not included in the past experience, though proceeding out of it by an orderly sequence of GROWTH. Therefore, since the divine cannot change its inherent nature, it must operate in the same manner within me; consequently, in my own special world, of which I am the center, it will move forward to produce new conditions, always in advance of any that have gone before." – Thomas Troward

Chapter VI. Sell Yourself on You!

"The self-image is the key to human personality and human behavior.   Change the self-image and you change the personality and behavior." – Maxwell Maltz

"This above all: to thine own self be true, and it must follow, as the night the day, thou canst not then be false to any man." - Shakespeare

Are you sold on you? Are you sold on how magnificent you are? If so, great! If you're not sure, keep reading. Acknowledging your magnificence is foundational to your success in selling. The strongest force of nature is man's desire to remain in alignment with his identity, his self-image, and the first question you might ask is, *who am I?*

Who do you think you are? Are you who you want to be, or are you what you've been told about yourself? You may say you are Amy Patterson or John Smith, but that's not who you are; your name is just your name. You might say *I am the CEO of ABC Company*, but that's just a position. Father, sister, brother, wife, son; these words describe your relationships. All of us engage in different roles, at work and at home.

What I want you to remember is your higher self, your spiritual essence—the spirit of you that flows through your heart when it's not blocked; the spiritual DNA in you that's perfect. As a baby, you looked around and recognized your family. You noticed your hand, or you stuck your finger in your mouth and bit down on it, only to realize that it was a part of you. You crawled across the floor and took your first step. You listened to mom and dad, then you spoke. You listened and observed and found meaning, or multiple meanings, for the same word. You took the first ride on the school bus and discovered the bench seats and some new friends, and the feeling of going over a bump and flying up in the air.

You watched people on bicycles, and you wanted one too. You learned how to ride your own bike and experienced freedom: the wind in your hair, and the fall, the scratches and brush burns. You learned through observation. You have physical, emotional, and mental experiences. But those experiences are not you. You are your consciousness, your awareness.

It's easy to be emotionally immersed in the drama, accepting that you're something that others think you are. Let me give you an example. I was cute as a button, with long blonde hair in first and second grade. I became immersed in school and even fantasized about being a teacher someday. Mom gave me a bulletin board, and I decorated it with construction paper and monthly themes, just like they did in school. Hearts for February, shamrocks for March. But by the time I reached the eighth grade, there was a bump on my nose. The Toni Tennille haircut was popular in the 1970s, and it seemed to accentuate the length of my nose and the bump. Was I cute as a button?

My brother Randy had his friends over to the house, and the boys had a field day. "Nose" is what they called me, not Rhonda. Nose. I was devastated, but I believed and accepted the idea that anyone who saw me, and my nose, thought it *was* me. I thought I was ruined because of my nose. This is a classic example of how a self-image gets created. You don't come into the world with a self-image. Something happens to you, though. People tell you things that trigger emotions, and you accept what they say as truth.

It's not truth, but you assume it is, so it becomes your truth. That's when your thermostat gets set. You act as if you're what everyone says (or thinks) you are.

God bless my parents. I told Mom and Dad how I felt, and my dad, my hero, found a plastic surgeon who suggested rhinoplasty surgery. In my second year of college, I had a nose job. When it was finished, I felt amazing! I thought my nose was attractive, that guys would talk to me, and that they'd entertain me as a possible girlfriend. And they did. I changed my self-image. Was I the same person? No, I was defined by my awareness, and it was limited.

So here I am, an unconscious competent. I shifted my self-image because of my changed appearance, but I never understood what caused the shift. I certainly wasn't conscious of how important this self-image thing was to success in selling.

Maxwell Maltz wrote a book called *Psycho-Cybernetics*. In that book, he explains that we can never outperform our self-image. Our self-image is like a cybernetic instrument that keeps us right where the setpoint is. What we believe or assume others think we are becomes our self-image. Think of it as your internal thermostat. Those assumptions govern your behavior and results. You have probably heard of set-points for managing your weight. You go on a diet and end up at the same weight. Why is that?

It's programming. No different than the cybernetic programming we find in airplanes, or the programming used in rockets sent to the moon. Your internal cybernetic instrument is your self-image, and it's fixed in your subconscious mind. The self-image is a fixed idea—it's an idea you engaged with on an emotional level, and it's habitual behavior. This statement is worth repeating again. "The self-image is not who you think you are, it is not who other people think you are; it is what you think other people think you are." And unless you're consciously aware of this and how to change it, nothing on the outside will change. It's an inside job. It is a block, a prison where you live, or it is your ticket to freedom. You get to choose.

Most of us fail to remember this fundamental principle. We fail to re-evaluate the ideas we accept. Most of our beliefs originate in the conditioning process of childhood when we seek love and approval. Conditioning causes people to suffer from approval addiction. We accept what the crowd tells us to be true. We rarely ask questions like, *where did my ideas come from? What ideas am I rejecting that I should accept? What ideas am I accepting that should be rejected?* We give our power away, or completely forget we have the power to think. We can choose to originate, accept, or reject ideas. Our beliefs, perceptions, attitude, and behaviors cause our life.

No wonder we can't break through our income glass ceiling or make a quantum leap forward. We focus on our results and on the effect, when we should be focused on belief, attitude, and perception, the things that cause our behavior. Unlike the duck that flies south, or the bear that sleeps every winter, or the trees that lose their leaves each fall, human beings can think and choose whether to accept or reject an idea. You have five senses, and you can originate new ideas with your creative mental faculties.

We have inductive reasoning—a way to create things through imagination; a way to shift our perceptions, to tap into intuition, to concentrate, to focus, to assemble thoughts into new ideas and concepts. But do they teach this in school? Unfortunately, not. Remember the movie the Matrix? The red and blue pill? Awareness is the ability to realize you can unplug yourself from the original programming and create your own program from within. You can live life on your terms.

Are you ready to wake up from the dream of your conditioning?

Let me share how the universe helped me to understand the importance of selling myself, courtesy of Rhonda's school of Hard Knocks. There is a way to break the glass, but it requires some things that appear to be illogical. Perhaps that's why so many of us remain stuck. It's taken me fifty-seven years to understand it. Watch for the emotional engagements and repetition that cause the shift.

At twenty-one I made the transition from college student and waitress to my first professional sales position as a chemical representative. I entered a predominantly male world back in 1985. I was 125 pounds with blond hair, dressed in a royal blue suit and royal blue high heels, and matching royal blue bangle earrings. Not exactly the picture of a sales professional that will come up in Google images, right? But that's how I dressed for my first day of sales calls.

That evening I attended a distributor training event. I made appointments that week and traveled with my sales manager for the first time. I didn't wear the same outfit all week, but the style of clothing was similar. By week's end, I was frustrated and feeling like the distributor reps and clients we met didn't take me seriously. There was nothing I wanted more than success, but I didn't feel like things were off to a good start.

God bless my first boss Bill for his honesty. He said, "Rhonda, can I be direct?" I said, "Yes, of course."

He said, "I think it's the way you're dressed. If you went to see a lawyer who was charging $250 an hour, how would you expect him to be dressed? In a T-shirt and jeans? Or would you expect him to be dressed in a nice suit, sitting behind a nice desk with a leather portfolio and Mont Blanc pen?"

Bill made his point: I needed to look professional, not casual. There are only two ways to change the self-image— either by emotional impact, or repetition. I was emotionally embarrassed. He suggested that I read *Dress for Success*. I wanted to succeed, I was coachable, and I did what he suggested. I went out and purchased a navy blue and black suit, and I adjusted the heels to a more conservative look. I practiced the sales presentation and became the woman I wanted to be. I acted like her. I earned respect because I changed the image. I exceeded sales targets for eight consecutive years, except for one year finishing at 98%.

When I transitioned to my next role at Applied Biosystems, my manager had complete confidence in my ability to handle consumable contracts and conversions. He spotted my interest and yearning to learn more. I was competent strategically and tactically on the selling of consumables. I just needed to develop competency on the science. I was lucky enough to get partnered up with my colleague and friend, who sold the instruments. She was a technical genius.

She taught me the basics of molecular biology in DNA Sequencing, DNA Synthesis, and QPCR. I did a ton of reading and study on molecular biology so I could establish technical rapport and trust with the scientists. This was a case of apprenticeship. Working with her on a weekly basis provided the repetition of hearing the presentations repeatedly. This autosuggestion transformed me and my confidence.

When I decided I wanted to become a manager, I re-learned how to adjust my self-image through failing. My manager at the time, received a promotion from District Manager to Regional Manager, and four of his direct reports, including me, interviewed for the role of District Manager. I didn't get that position, and it charged me emotionally. I went through the grieving process. But the VP of Sales was honest with me. He said, "Rhonda, if you want to be a manager, you need to act like one."

I said, "What do you mean?"

He told me, "When we choose managers, we get input from multiple managers. How you *show up* at district meetings, regional meetings, and national meetings matters. Ask yourself, do you support the leadership in meetings, or do you congregate with your colleagues and complain? Are you leading the team from where you are by example, without a title?"

This is the same advice I would hear later in life: "Act as if you are the person you want to become. Walk, talk, follow, and lead like her. Don't wait for a title, be that person now."

I learned a lesson about the law of perpetual transformation. But here's the thing about being an unconscious competent, or unconscious incompetent: if you don't understand the principle behind what's happening, you'll relearn it again and again.

I left Applied Biosystems in 2004 and slid into an individual contributor role at Agencourt Biosciences. I had to adjust. The selling part was easy, but the technical competency for sample prep and sequencing services had to be learned. After a year, I was back in the manager role covering the east coast. A good manager to work for is a business partner, always supporting you with respect and that's what I had at the time. We had a great time building up the team and growing the business from $10 million to $40 million. In 2008 we reaped the rewards for our efforts. Beckman Coulter bought Agencourt, and we cashed in on the profit earned from our stock options. Of course, change occurred with the transition of ownership, and by 2010 I was again faced with a need for a self-image adjustment.

My manager's position was eliminated and he left the company. That day, a huge cold sore appeared on my lip. The saboteur judge voice inside me let me know we were under attack. It's amazing how fear can stop you in your tracks. I became the North American Director of Sales with fourteen direct reports. At the end of that year, Beckman decided to roll all my direct reports into individual contributor roles under the Diagnostics and Life Sciences divisions, which meant there was no need for my role. I remember asking the VP of Molecular Diagnostics, "Then what do you need me for?" Talk about a struggle to maintain one's identity. I thought I was the director of that business, and in one swift second, poof, that role was gone!

I interviewed for a Diagnostic Area Director position, an opportunity to manage managers. I didn't get the job, and I can see now that it was because my setpoint wasn't adjusted. My thermostat was set on the Regional Manager/Director position that had evaporated. When you're feeling sorry for yourself, you can't see opportunity. The Korn Ferry leadership assessment I took confirmed that my self-image was stagnant. The assessment tagged me emotionally in the role of managing direct reports, not managers.

It reported exactly where my self-image set point was. And this is the price of ignorance. I was unaware that my internal thermostat was projecting Regional Manager, not Area Director. I lost the opportunity because I failed to make the self-image adjustment. Consciously and logically, I believed I could do the job, but I hadn't developed the belief emotionally. I wasn't on the frequency of being a confident area director in that interview.

It's true: your internal emotional image controls your vibration, your body, and your results. This unconscious incompetence causes your life until your awareness expands to understand that you *can* control and adjust the outcome. The price you must pay forward is study.

There's hope that an unconscious competent and unconscious incompetent can become consciously aware of what's going on and take their power back. When the student is ready, the teacher will appear. It was during the transition from working full-time in corporate America to becoming a full-time entrepreneur in 2019 that I learned how to become a conscious competent. I learned how to adjust my internal thermostat and my self-image. I've always said, "If you can learn to sell salt, a basic commodity, you can sell anything." That's true, if you learn how to adjust your self-image.

By 2019 I was in my nineteenth year of sales management. As you can imagine, I had some habits! On Monday April 10th of that year, my job was eliminated. I was at a trade show with a new sales representative, week 2 of Q2. After lunch, the new representative received a phone call from his manager and told me to call HR. I wondered what was up. I called her and she said, "We've made some hard decisions, and your position has been eliminated."

In 2017 I had completed my coaching certification. Coaching is what I love to do, and I knew that I would run my own business someday, I just didn't expect to be running my business so quickly. I looked up in the sky after digesting the news and said, "Okay, God, I guess you want me to do this now." I made the decision that morning to become an entrepreneur. I needed to grow, to do something different that I hadn't done before. I entered the personal development field as a coach.

I knew I wanted to stay in the sales arena. I loved sales and salespeople, and I didn't want to lose touch with that community. I also decided I wanted to become a speaker, and that I would provide sales training services and coaching services to support sales teams and executives. I was consumed with things like setting up a website, designing the training programs, and coaching packages *before* I really understood who I wanted to become.

I needed order where order didn't exist, and that was in my mind. My self-image was stuck on the old thermostat of Area Sales Director with thirty-five years of corporate sales experience. By September, I had my first clients established, but I needed help. I heard about Bob Proctor on an audio tape by Steve Siebold called *177 Secrets for Mental Toughness*. Steve referred to Bob Proctor as "The Toronto Thunder." I googled Bob Proctor, found his website, and requested some information. Later that week I received a call from the Proctor

Gallagher Institute in response to my inquiry, and I made a decision that changed the trajectory of my life.

I made an investment in myself and my business to attend the Matrix event in Toronto that July. The Matrix is a service Bob Proctor offers for new entrepreneurs. It's a resourceful environment where people from all over the world come to collaborate, mastermind, and explore opportunities for financial independence through multiple sources of income. The experience was transformational.

For the first time in fifty-six years, I discovered the concept of having multiple sources of income. When I left, I had settled on an avatar: I would work with salespeople and provide sales training services. I wanted to return to the corporate world and be a change agent for unveiling the greatest asset corporations have, their employees. I decided to become a certified consultant for the Proctor Gallagher Institute and their program *Thinking Into Results*. The concept behind *Thinking Into Results* is to create awareness of how to change results by changing behavior.

Corporations spend millions of dollars gathering information, yet behaviors don't change. Proctor's philosophy is based on natural laws. Change the cause, change the effect. The habits of a salesperson (cause) create sales commissions (effect). That resonated with me. I wanted to help transform corporate culture to value its employees, to understand that people are the greatest assets a company has. Since I didn't have my own corporate program, it made sense for me to become an affiliate and facilitate Bob's materials. I studied the lessons continuously and became a product of the product. This was the beginning of my journey into the personal development business.

So, here's the rub. You must fully understand what you are selling and why. People don't buy merchandise; they buy what the merchandise does for them. Logically, I had bought into the concepts of Bob Proctor's program. But emotionally, my self-image wasn't changed. I didn't understand the powerful pull that self-image had on me, and I had no idea how to change it. It was like baking a cake without the egg and the baking powder. My self-image said, "Who do you think you are? All you've ever done is work in the corporate world as a sales director." My self-image was worried about what everyone would think.

And my beliefs about how to study held me back. I've always been a curious learner who gathers up tons of information—the classic self-help queen. I wasn't being a good follower. I wasn't applying myself with the repetition and emotional impact because it seemed illogical, and it was. My old beliefs governed my behavior. I needed to get order in my mind. Who was I becoming? What did I want?

One of my mentors at the Proctor Gallagher Institute told me a truth, a truth I didn't want to believe. He said, "Just because you were a rock star selling one product, doesn't guarantee you are going to be a rock star selling this product. Success is not permanent." Did you ever hear something like that? Something that causes you to say, "Well I'll show you!"

I started making calls. I practiced and failed repeatedly. I couldn't figure out what was missing. My confidence was low, and I wasn't sure of myself. In hindsight I can see I was being mechanical. I wasn't in the spirit of Bob Proctor's program, and I didn't comprehend what I was selling. But you can't rush understanding. You must apply the knowledge to truly learn.

Reading a book or listening to a lesson will not change your behavior. You'll gather knowledge, but until you apply it and use it, and even fail with it, you won't develop understanding or "knowing." I attended the consultant's training in September, but by October I was still in the fog. My beliefs and perception of myself hadn't changed. I was unsure of myself, and I needed help.

There's a great book called *The Prosperous Coach*, by Steve Chandler and Rich Litvin. The book says you're a hypocrite if you're a coach and don't have a coach. Ouch. I did some networking and heard a coach speak in a Mastermind session I attended. Everything he said resonated with me. I knew he was the one, so I reached out.

I'll never forget the first conversation. Dave said to me, "I know what your problem is. You have no order in your mind.

I can help you get that order." Up to that point, I was doing the same thing I'd done all my life. Shelf help. Reading. Gathering information. I was holding onto that old idea. My old beliefs controlled my reasoning. It wasn't logical to write out goals every day. It wasn't logical to read and listen to lessons again and again. It wasn't logical to talk to myself through autosuggestion every day. It wasn't logical to visualize three times a day.

It took me eight months to accept and recognize the fact I wasn't emotionally involved with changing my self-image. And then it finally sunk in. Vibration is altered by feeling. I needed to act as if I was her, the woman I decided to become. I had to burn my bridges and leave my old self-image behind.

That day I made the decision to have a new belief, and I allowed myself to accept the new ideas and receive the rewards. I went to see an image consultant. I joined a mastermind group, made list of people I admired, and I did the work. I took my power back. And it changed my life. People noticed the shift. I had become her: the new independent woman, the business owner who made a difference in peoples' lives. Today I am consciously causing my life and my sales, consciously causing my results. You can do the same.

Beliefs and assumptions are nothing more than ideas you accept, either through the lens of courage and creativity, or through the lens of conformity and competition. Attitude is the composite of your thoughts, feelings, and actions. Perception is the lens through which you view your life. Behaviors are a direct reflection of the ideas you become emotionally involved in. These beliefs, perceptions, and attitudes cause all the results in your life.

Faith is all there is. Faith is a function of your will power. The question is, are you consciously choosing your beliefs, attitude, perception, and behaviors? What percentage of the time are you on autopilot? How often are you questioning your beliefs and perceptions, and how do they shape your attitude and behavior? All beliefs serve us. The question to ask yourself is, "How am I benefiting from this belief? How often am I truly thinking and utilizing my power to purposely cause my life?"

Now, you may be wondering, if I haven't done this before, how am I going to build up my confidence and change my self-image to sell well? If you really want a breakthrough, I highly recommend you accept the idea of hiring a coach. I have three of them: one for mindset, one for specialized knowledge on being a speaker-author, and a third for health and relationships. Mentorship is the transference of knowledge and, more important, belief. We all need direction, and the perfect coach exists for you.

To sell well, consider accepting the idea that selling is an infinite game of transformation. The room for self-improvement is the largest room in the world. There are three components you can use to build up your confidence:

1) Self-Image

2) Develop your strengths.

3) Look for the good in everyone you meet.

Ask yourself who you want to become. Who is it that everyone should think you are? How do you want to show up? How does this person walk, talk, lead, collaborate, create, and live? Who do they hang out with, what legacy do they leave behind, and what stewardship standards do they want to adopt? What are you willing to give, or give up, to get it? Get yourself into an environment that is conducive to your unfoldment. The people in your life influence your vibration.

Next, *act as if* you are that person. Prepare as if it is already so. Stop living life based on what you think others think you are. Decide what *you think* others think you are.

Energy is never created or destroyed. It is manipulated to create new forms by a change in vibrational frequency. So, remember the feeling is the secret. When you act in a state of expectancy, you operate on a new frequency where your goal and confidence reside; you have applied faith. Confidence starts with decision making. The more confidently you make decisions on your own, without worry or need of approval from others, the faster you will build up that confidence. Yes, new roles are uncomfortable, but that's how we grow and expand. Get comfortable being uncomfortable. Embrace being uncomfortable; it is your gateway to freedom.

Develop your strengths. What is it that you do well, and how can you do it better? It amazes me how quickly we as human beings want to "take it easy," whatever that means. We have talents, but we forget to use another gift we have, our time. The question is, do you invest time or spend it? I believe use of time is one of the greatest opportunities for salespeople. If you measure how much time you invest in selling, calling, contacting, following up, and persuading, you'd find the percentage of time used in the best way to be quite small. Forbes Magazine did a study in 2017, and the statistics showed that the actual time spent on selling during a day was less than thirty percent!

If you made just a ten percent shift in time investment over a year, you would cause a quantum leap in your sales performance. Your strengths are your gifts. Going back to the law of use, ask yourself, "How well am I investing my talents, time, and my mind on a daily basis?" If you ask that question, I am confident you will hit a golden vein of opportunity for yourself. Develop your strengths and watch your confidence rise.

Finally, look for the good in everyone you meet. That one might sound peculiar to you. What does that have to do with building up my confidence? It's rather genius, and here's why. What we see in others is a mirror of ourselves. When you look for the good in others, you will see the good in yourself, and your confidence will grow and expand. If you look for what is lacking, you will reflect what is lacking in yourself. That's why Dale Carnegie's golden rule is to never condemn, criticize, or complain. Whatever we give our focus and attention to will grow. If we want to build up our confidence, we become a good finder.

Just that one perception shift can make all the difference. The law of polarity states that there is always a positive and negative to everything in life. You can only focus on one thing at a time. Choose wisely and ask what you would like to grow.

Your confidence? Well then, the best recipe is to look for the good!

I hope the stories of my growth, transformation, and experiences will provide you with insight and help get you into the spirit of selling—to sell more, and to easily adjust through the transitions that occur on your journey. It all begins with an examination of the ideas you choose to accept or reject. Consider this: it's likely that you don't know a lot of things, so allow yourself the space to think. If you reflect on all the major transformations you've had in your life, you might recognize that the greatest successes occurred because you accepted a new idea.

Realize and accept what a magnificent human being you are. There is an image of perfection that is perfect in you; it is resident in all human beings. The more we move in the direction of that image, the more our life will improve. There is no end to the good you can experience as you develop greater awareness of the perfection that lies within you. Internal self-image adjustment is the magical switch that moves us in the direction of that perfection. Decide on who you want to become this year. Make that decision, and more of your potential will rise to the surface. Sell yourself on you!

For more resources to reset your self-image, go to www.thespiritofselling.com

Chapter VII – Amateurs Compete –

Professionals Create.

The Law of Perpetual Transmutation and The Law of Pure Potentiality

"There's a difference between interest and commitment. When you are interested in something, you do it only when it's convenient. When you're committed to something, you accept no excuses, only results." – Ken Blanchard

"Competition is ego. Cooperation is spirit."—Steve Siebold, author, 177 Mental Toughness Secrets

"He who masters others is wise. He who masters himself is enlightened." – Lao Tzu

"Masters have confidence in their ability to acquire, grow, and perform to the highest levels."   – Dave Conway, Conway Consulting

How does the word master or mastery make you feel? Do you resonate with the word? I don't know about you, but I love the idea of learning how to master myself through study. Just how much potential can I bring to the surface?

How do you bring more potential to the surface? Create, of course! If you decide to become a master at selling, get ready for an infinite game of creation that will bring you adventure, fulfillment, and joy. While some think it's hard, I say it's easier to win. Let's dive in and find out why.

Here is the first idea I'd like you to consider and evaluate: competition and comparison *with others* are a complete waste of time. The pros prefer to use their time and effort to create value for those they serve. The pros know that the only competition is with your own ignorance. Awareness is what they seek. The journey is an infinite game, and humility is your ally. The pros always create something new; they only compete with themselves and their previous results. They set high standards and hold themselves accountable. They learn and look for new ways to expand their awareness. They deliberately move on a path toward mastery.

Movies like *The Matrix* illustrate how a person can master himself with conscious choice. Red pill or blue pill – which is better? Free your mind? Or live-in blissful ignorance following the masses? I think some of us are born with an innate desire to stand out. Look at Michael Jordan in the *Last Dance* documentary. He's competing with himself. Jordan said, "Whatever it takes, at any cost." He demonstrated his willingness to sacrifice whatever it takes. That's the attitude of a professional.

There is a cost. Every time you engage in selling someone on doing something for themselves, you're asking them to make a sacrifice. You sacrifice every day, whether you realize it or not. You're sacrificing your time to read this book. And your desires are always coming into form. That might be a hard pill to swallow, but it's true.

Since every choice brings a sacrifice, a good question to ask yourself is, "What meaning do I place on the word sacrifice?" Whatever meaning you have for it, your customer is picking up what you're putting down. For example, if you believe the only prerequisite to decide is *want*, then your customer will pick up on that feeling. If you believe that people evaluate and make decisions based on what they have, or that it's hard to let go of what they have for something better, they'll pick that up, too. Your thought is powerful.

I used to cringe at the word sacrifice. I thought about Bible stories and animals on altars, but that's not what it's about. I used to associate sacrifice with a loss instead of a win. What about you? What is your definition of sacrifice? Today I see sacrifice as the way I make room for transformation—room for a miracle. There is a law of prosperity that says nature abhors a vacuum, so everything is always full. If you want something new in your life, you need to make space for it. Make space for the miracles. It could be a trade of one habit for a more empowering one. A new idea to replace the old one. Sacrifice is removing something of a lower nature and replacing it with something of a higher nature. Who wouldn't want to play that game?

Remember what you're really selling. You are selling your clients on an idea that you want them to accept, adopt, or approve. You're selling them on the benefits of your product or service. That means your client will need to sacrifice their complacency and leave the shore to sail toward their promised land. They either move or stay stuck. In Miller Heiman strategic selling, the Blue Sheet requires you to denote the buying mode – is the buyer in growth mode? Trouble mode? Even keel? Or overconfident?

Mode gives you clues for the motive, the reason for doing something or moving in a new direction. When you sell and persuade, you're asking your client to decide, which is the opposite of procrastination. You're asking them to sacrifice an investment of their time and money for your product or service.

If you're not complacent, and if you're decisive—if you're willing to sacrifice whatever it takes, then you'll have an easy time helping your clients to do the same. If you procrastinate and have become complacent, chances are you'll let yourself and your prospective client off the hook. Why? Because you can't give another human being something you don't have.

You might not like what I'm about to say, but I'm going to say it anyway. Any objection you or I experience in selling is because the client was in harmony with something we were thinking. The better you become at raising your standards, making decisions, and sacrifice, the easier it will be for you to help clients have the confidence to do the same.

School teaches us about competition via sports and economics class. In economics, competition is a scenario where different economic firms are in contention to obtain goods that are limited by varying the elements of the marketing mix: price, product, promotion and place. In sports we compete against the other teams in the league. There are winners, losers, and a scorecard at every event. The question is, where does the player or the firm focus their attention? Do they compare themselves with their performance in the last game? Or with the other team?

When I started in sales, my knowledge was limited to what I learned in school and in life—and from watching football games. At my first job with J.T. Baker, our largest distributor was VWR Scientific, and they sold two lines of chemicals, J.T. Baker and EM Science. When you sell through distribution, it's an infinite game of mindshare and relationships. Distributors carry thousands of products, and the objective is how can you get and keep the distributor's attention. You need the distributor to sell your products, even when you're not there. The benefit of a strong relationship with your distribution partner is like multiplying your efforts.

Our VP of sales viewed EM Science as our nemesis, and our sales meetings might have worked in a football locker room. Get pumped to win the game! Go after the competition and *eat their lunch.* I was a rookie, and I took that seriously. Using the word nemesis puts you in a state of enmity. The animal instincts to fight or flight come in. The cortisol surge can give you a temporary energy rush, but it usually doesn't help you to go the distance.

I remember meeting the EM representative at my first dealer training. His name was Dave, and he was winning awards. I figured he was eating my lunch, and I was losing. Not a very empowering attitude. But Dave was just a nice guy who did things in a certain way. He followed the golden rule. He was an active listener who listened with his emotions. That's why he was successful. He wasn't competing or stressed, he was focused on creating value.

Eventually, I learned that thinking about Dave eating my lunch was a waste of time and energy. I moved my focus back to what I could control. I focused on what I could do to take my game to the next level. I learned to do what he was doing, which was live by the golden rule. My relationships with the distributors improved. I focused on helping them win. If I lost a deal, I learned from it and refused to make the same mistake twice. As a result, I exceeded my plan seven out of the eight years there. It's easier to win when you move your focus off what the competition is doing and unto what you can do to create more value.

Economics classes discuss demand and supply curves in macro and microeconomics. The textbooks say there's a fixed pie of supply, the total available market; that businesses in the same industry must compete for market share. But that's a limited concept. That theory assumes there will be no new creation. Look at how fast things changed with phones, from the time of Alexander Graham Bell's invention to Steve Jobs' introduction of the iPhone. At first, wires carried frequencies for the phones. Remember the rotary phones on the wall in your mom's kitchen? Or the shared line at the general store on the TV show *Green Acres*?

When I started my sales career in 1985, we made sales calls from hotel lobbies. You would stand in the phone booth, punch in the number you were calling, and follow that with a phone credit card number. Hotel lobbies had banks of phones, and you had to get there early. In the 1990s they invented the bag phones for your car—still wired, but mobile. Then came the wireless technology for mobile flip phones. After the internet and email got active, the Blackberry was invented as the way to go—just one device on the road.

Apple turned Blackberry on its head, though. Our phones do everything now. Who knows what's next? In the 1960s, Napoleon Hill wrote about a congressman at the turn of the century who wanted to introduce a bill to close the patent office—there was nothing else to be patented, said the congressman. But that's laughable. Change is swift, and the illusion of a fixed pie becomes obsolete with every new creation. The pie isn't fixed! Change is happening faster than ever, and the best strategy is to create value, your value. The pros know this.

There are sales professionals in the marketplace, and there are amateurs. The pros are always raising their standards. If they're making one sale in a week, they try to figure out how to make a sale each day. If they are selling one product per sale, they figure out how to sell two or three. If they're selling $1000 packages, they're asking how they can sell $5000 dollar packages. Or $50,000 dollar packages. They're always thinking, always asking questions. They have a perpetual longing, a dissatisfaction with the status quo. They always want more. Universal Law and nature work the same way.

So, why don't we have more professionals? What holds a person back from becoming a pro? It's ignorance. Lack of awareness. Remember? Earlier in the book we discussed the fact that we are not our thoughts, our emotions, our names, or our roles. We are our awareness. To gain mastery over oneself, awareness needs to grow and expand. Russell Conwell, who founded Temple University, was the man who wrote a book called *Acres of Diamonds.*

Conwell's story illustrates how ignorance robs us of our potential. If you're not familiar with the book, it is a true story of an African farmer named Ali, who heard the tales of diamond miners who had struck it rich. Ali left his family and farm in Africa to search for new land that would provide him those riches. He never found the diamonds. He grew old, became despondent, and threw himself in a river and drowned. He committed suicide.

The new owner of Ali's farm noticed a blue flash of light in the creek, one day. He picked up the crystalline rock figure that sparkled in the water. He put it on the fireplace mantel and forgot about it until a visitor told him it was a diamond. That farm became one of the largest diamond mines in the world. Ali had been sitting on acres of diamonds, right in his backyard, but he didn't recognize the diamonds in the rough. Our only competition is our ignorance. Do you look outside of yourself for answers? Do you think you know all there is to know? Do you ever think that sometimes pastures look greener because they're getting better care?

Ali's problem was that he lacked the skills and qualities to recognize what a diamond looks like in its rough state. He lacked awareness. How many times are we like Ali? Walking away from challenges that are opportunities and gifts in disguise? Not willing to develop and refine our skills? Thinking we know all there is? Thinking the grass is greener in another pasture and not recognizing the diamonds in our own backyard?

Not asking ourselves, "What's good here? Or, what can I do with this?"

Dr. Conwell was a minister in Philadelphia when a group of boys came to him and asked about the opportunity to get a college education. Dr. Conwell didn't let the current state of affairs (or lack of funds) control his thinking. Instead, Dr. Conwell saw the opportunity in the rough. He recognized a problem and turned it into an opportunity. He didn't allow his thoughts to be controlled by the existing results.

He asked himself questions, and he thought. He went to the workshop of his imagination, formed new thoughts, got emotionally engaged with a creative idea, and acted. He delivered more than six-thousand lectures on *Acres of Diamonds* and raised $7 Million dollars to fund and found Temple University. Dr. Conwell focused on creating value. It's easier to win when you decide to create.

So, what characteristics do the real sales pros possess? I would say the pros have *grit*; they make decisions, and they finish what they start. They choose a degree of excellence; the willingness and desire to reveal the brilliance from the diamond in the rough. That diamond in the rough is their awareness. Think about that: the sales pros know their potential exists within; they want to express it, and they are willing to undergo pressure, to be cut, polished, and purified, to reveal the brilliance inside. They do that by expanding their awareness. The only person they compete with is themselves. They know the game is internal and infinite. They continually ask themselves, "How can I take my game to the next level?" The pros are champions because they have unbounded creativity.

It's not until we undergo some pressure, some cuts, and challenges that we start to see our sparkle within. There is no such thing as failure in life, just lessons. The only failure is when you quit. Think of a time when you've been in a real pinch, and then you start thinking. Really thinking. And then you discover something inside you that you never saw before. You pull the rip cord. You say to yourself, "No more." Or "I'm going for it, no matter what it takes."

That decision to make it happen flips you onto another thought frequency you haven't visited before. You apply action to your ideas, and your awareness expands, just like that. You discover something within that you didn't know you had. And once you have it, it's yours forever. Every time you expand your awareness, you win!

When we arrive on the planet, our awareness is in a rough state, just like a diamond. The more we develop awareness, the more we expand and grow. Psychology states there are seven levels of awareness for humans. Nature seems to like the number seven.

The first level of human awareness is **Animal Consciousness** – the animal instinct for survival. At this level, an individual is dependent, reacts to situations, circumstances, and people outside of themselves. The individual operates by fight or flight. Thought, at this level, is dominated by the outside world. This is our survival instinct to protect ourselves from attack. We react.

The second level of awareness is **Mass Consciousness,** for a sense of belonging. This is the game of *Monkey See, Monkey Do.* The mass consciousness is heavily influenced by the environment. Earl Nightingale used to say, "If you see the masses walking in one direction, go in the other." Mass awareness is where conformity develops, based on the desire for approval and love. Only three to five percent of the population move past this level of awareness.

Going back to the Matrix analogy, many prefer to live in blissful ignorance while following the masses. Benjamin E. Mays made a wise statement, one worth remembering. He said, *"The tragedy in life is not found in failure, but complacency. Not in doing too much, but in doing too little. Not in you living above your means, but below your capacity. It's not the failure, but aiming too low that is life's greatest tragedy."* My hope and intention for you in selling is that you consciously choose to aim high.

For some, there is no sense of fulfillment in the mass consciousness. They become curious and tired of the *Monkey*

See Monkey Do game. The individual gets an urge for something different. They move to the third level of human awareness, which is characterized by **Aspirations**. The individual focuses on self-esteem and achievement. Here, awareness expands, but the individual is reluctant to act and sacrifice, to pay the price. They live in the state of hope and wishing. If you truly want a different result, you must be willing to pay the price. If you choose to stay in the comfort zone, this is as far as you will ever go.

The fourth level of human awareness is focused on the **Individual,** what makes you unique. The individual's ideas move them into action, and the individual experiences feedback. Self-esteem, confidence, and self-worth emerge. Sometimes, the feedback from taking that action can sting, but the pros know feedback is the breakfast of champions! Like Edison would say, "I never failed, I just discovered multiple ways that did not work."

The fifth level of awareness is **Self-discipline**, the ability to give yourself a command and follow it. When one reaches this state, they know they will require the tool of self-discipline to gain more awareness. Self-discipline is the art of choosing actions that are in your own best interest. Will Smith describes self-discipline as self-love. You forgo short-term pleasure in exchange for self-respect. You take full control of your mind.

For example, Will says things to himself like, "Dude I know this pizza looks good, but I can't let you eat that because it will make you feel like crap. I love you too much to let you do that." Self-esteem is not about what other people think, it's about how you feel about you. It's the recognition that you don't need anyone else's approval, you just need yours. You learn to love yourself and recognize how magnificent you are. You are willing to sacrifice the crowd approval to be uniquely you.

At the sixth level, **Experience** awareness, the individual begins to learn by taking massive action. It's the repetition, the application of the self-discipline, that increases the experiences, the confidence, and faith in themselves. The individual is engaged and connecting with others through meaning and purpose. The individual realizes that all success involves having a pleasing personality and alliances. Those alliances will be more effective if they're built on a foundation of harmony and cooperation.

The seventh level of awareness is **Mastery,** whereby superior understanding of a particular subject or ability resides. Confidence soars, and humility is observed as essential. Every master has a servant. In mastery, you take full control of your conscious mind, with its inductive reasoning and the power of choice. Your conscious mind is the master; your subconscious emotional mind is your servant. You, as the master, also become the servant. Every time you make a sale, you're finding more people to serve.

How does this path towards greater awareness tie into Universal Law? One of the most basic dynamic laws of life says that *we either create or disintegrate.* Nothing ever stays the same or stays at rest. The Law of Perpetual Transmutation states that energy in the universe is always transmuting into and out of form. Energy cannot stay still. Energy = Mass x the speed of light squared. Thought can travel at the speed of light. Thought is what can transmute and shape energy into power or form.

When you become the master of your conscious mind, you create, live, and thrive. If you give that power away, you disintegrate. Energy and mass are the same thing, just in two different forms: one invisible, the other visible. When you create, you shape energy by concentrating it; you grow, you move forward.

The Laws of the Universe apply to the marketplace, just like they apply in nature. If you aren't dissatisfied or longing for something, you're not going forward. There is no neutral, and you never arrive. You're always moving. The question is, in what direction? You either go forward or slide backwards. Your stock value in the marketplace either goes up or goes down. The more value you create in the marketplace, the more valuable you are to the marketplace. Write that down and absorb it because it's a law.

Dissatisfaction and longing are the greatest motivators for growth; they are your creative vibrations. Your creativity is the way you can leave others with the impression of increase and serve them. There is a tremendous difference between saying, "I'm going to do something…" and actually doing it. There's a difference between thinking of starting a project and starting it; a difference between recognizing an opportunity and acting on it.

Creation requires action. It comes down to possessing an attitude of excellence: taking action, and not just when it's convenient. Ask yourself, "How many ideas do I have on a daily basis to take my game to the next level, impact my sales funnel, and close more deals?" And "How many of those ideas am I acting on?" Be brutally honest with yourself. Are you executing those ideas with persistence, to see it come to pass? And how many times are you saying, "I will as soon as…?" Do you drift and let yourself off the hook? Do you finish what you start? What would you need to believe to stay focused on your mastery?

I can't tell you how many people I've met who are shocked when they find that their position has been eliminated.

It's these types of setbacks or sufferings that help set us up for more. To be honest, I think getting fired, at least once, will teach you a great lesson. Getting fired helps you realize if you're in the right place, if you're doing something you love. It reinforces lessons about universal law. If we don't learn the lesson, the lesson will keep repeating itself. Suffering has a great way of expanding our awareness, of waking us up out of our complacency.

Organizations thrive based on harmony. I can't list all the reasons sales positions become eliminated; however, I can tell you the most common reasons. Complacency is at the top of the list. No doubt, complacency causes replacement. Earl Nightingale said, "The opposite of courage is not cowardice, it is complacency." When a corporation is in high growth mode, you can hide for a while and be complacent. You can do the minimum to slide by, but it won't last long.

The day that company hits a bump in the road, goes through a merger or acquisition, gains a new CEO, goes through a cycle of recession, or encounters a new competitor, there is no more hiding. These scenarios are when the pros are needed the most. They are also the scenarios that force companies to cut and eliminate the dead wood.

If a decision is made to reduce the force, the managers will be asked rank their teams based on performance. The low performers who have been complacent, the ones who are not creating value, will be let go. The pros will always have a job, either with that company, or with another one who recognizes their stock value. It shouldn't be a surprise; it's the law.

Beyond complacency, those who inhibit harmony within the organization will cause their own demise. Conflict and attitude issues cause people to be fired all the time. Conflict issues typically occur when an individual's values are challenged, or someone's feelings get hurt and they take it personally. These people form an internal competition against something or someone. Mother Theresa shared some wisdom when she said, "I will never march against something or someone. I will only march for something or someone."

Forming opposition to someone in a company is not an empowering or sustaining strategy. There will be a winner and a loser, and the loser, eventually, will be you. The pros don't play those games. There's nothing wrong with healthy debates, but when you don't seek to understand before being understood, or if you don't express your views in a respectful manner; if you adopt the *I'll show you* attitude instead of applying the golden rule, your bank account with the other will move into the red. They say one negative interaction will require three positive deposits to eliminate it. Great companies understand this.

When communication is suppressed, engagement lessens, and separation sets in. The root cause of this problem is absence of emotional intelligence or awareness. This is the *I'm right, you are wrong* syndrome, and the stubborn suffer. If no one wants to be around you, it's because your attitude is a drain. When you get dismissed for a bad attitude, or the inability to work in harmony, the company won't offer an explanation. You might hear things like, "We have made a decision to change direction." Or "We've made a decision to terminate our relationship."

Cooperation makes it easier to win.

The last thing that causes disintegration is ego imbalance. I used to think ego was all bad, but I was only looking at one side of it. Ego can be both positive and negative since the law of polarity applies. There is no willpower without ego. Ego is the seat of the will; it serves as the supreme court in your mind. Salespeople need willpower. Willpower is your ability to focus and concentrate on something. Sales pros must have an empathy/ego balance.

The empathy attribute is the ability to emotionally listen, to understand the client. The ego attribute is needed to tell the client the truth and get them to act. If you don't have an ego, you won't push for change and persuade the client. The pros can sit with the client with empathy and ego. It's a balancing act. The ego becomes a problem when it gets up on a perch and separates itself from others on the couch. That's when you'll experience the extreme punishment from natural law.

I learned this myself through the school of hard knocks. After ten years of service with a company and being told I walked on water, and how wonderful I was, I was asked to fill in for the VP of Sales while she was on maternity leave. My ego had me on a perch. We had an individual at the time who wasn't performing well, and I was asked to remedy the situation. Impatient, my ego decided to try and force things. My ego was out of balance: too much ego, not enough empathy. The individual was put on a performance improvement plan.

Well, force is not power, and force negates. Instead of practicing empathy and respecting the individual, and instead of listening, I used my ego. Well, let me tell you, nature gave me an ass kicking. The individual filed complaints against me with HR that required investigations. At that time, there was restructuring going on, and I manifested an HR issue that cost me my job. This was a classic case of backfire and karma. I was not following the golden rule of respect, and as a result, I lost mine.

There are no mistakes in life, only lessons. There were two things I learned; it was time for me to leave. I had become complacent and was not growing and expanding for my purpose. My heart was not into pursuing a VP position in a large organization. I always wanted my own business. Second, and most important, I learned that respect for all humanity is always paramount, and humility is essential. Always follow the golden rule.

So why is the path of a pro easier to win? It takes just as much energy to experience abundance and prosperity as it does to experience scarcity and poverty. Focus on what you can control, which is you. We were not made for work; work was made for us to express our uniqueness. If you don't love what you're doing, you're not in harmony with your work. Get in the flow of natural law, and always be in harmony.

You can't be the best version of yourself if you're focused on a low vibration energy, doing what you don't want to do. If you fall in love with what you do, you can't help but to experience harmony, growth, and the desire to perpetually expand and express your gifts. Success is a natural consequence of doing something you love.

Don't stay in a job you hate, or one that isn't allowing you to play to your strengths and grow. Find something that you will love. Ask, is this job worthy of me? You're trading your life for it. Choose a position where you can utilize your massive creative abilities and gifts to continually create value. The reward is fulfillment, joy, and adventure.

So, if you agree with the idea that comparison and competition with others is a waste of time, and you want to work toward mastery, to become a professional, what character traits are worth considering for adoption? I believe the pros have grit. Temple's students are taught the meaning and mantra of grit. Merriam Webster's definition of grit is *"firmness of character; indomitable spirit."* I like that definition.

Remember, we're talking about *The Spirit of Selling!* Forbes published an article on the five-character qualities of grit in October of 2015: *Courage, Conscientious, Resilience,*

Excellence, & Follow through. Let's look at how they apply to sales.

Sales Pros have the courage of a missionary. They make regular investments in study, thinking, and planning time. They follow up with action and a sense of urgency. Urgency is not hurry and fear – it is planned action with purpose. Sales pros don't quit or take things personally. They understand that there's a difference between "No, not now," and "No, never!" They form the habit of doing things that failures don't like to do. And their motto is "Do It Now!" They are focused on the results.

Sales pros are conscientious. They remember that without consciousness they don't have choice. They're careful, diligent, and orderly. They want to do things well. They take obligations to others seriously and tend to be efficient and organized. Clients learn to rely on their integrity.

Sales pros are resilient. They bounce back into shape, no matter how many times they get knocked down. Like a diamond, they absorb pressure, and their brilliance surfaces. They are persistent. They have faith in themselves. They are influenced by the desire for pleasing results, while failures are influenced by pleasing methods.

Excellence is a choice the pros make. They evaluate their own character, commit to finishing what they start, and continually raise their standards. Standards are the mortar for the entire structure. Without standards, you lose expectation. You accept what is and start to settle. If you settle, you can't go any farther.

The pros follow up. The Law of Circulation in the sales cycle is to prospect, present, and follow up. Without a robust follow up system, salespeople miss opportunities. Customers know, appreciate, and respect the sales pros who call a second time. And a third. It demonstrates the care they can expect after the sale takes place.

Steven Covey said the difference between the pros and the amateurs is in their ability to respond. *"Response-ability."* Masters respond. The pros learn to take subjective control of their mind and their perceptions. They sit in the seat of awareness, watch, and contemplate. Instead of reacting, they respond.

The Law of Pure Potentiality reminds us of how to access pure consciousness. There is more awareness through silence, meditation, and non-judgement. Simply put, "Be Present." When the mind is quiet in meditation and not distracted by thoughts and external noise, all that's left is the higher self and no-thing. Here in the silence, you can fuse with the power that is and experience the bliss of pure potentiality.

Every human being on the planet starts out in a rough state. Opportunities for us to expand that awareness are everywhere if we only start to look for them. The question is how many of us will remember that our true essence is divine, that we are unique, and that we don't need to compete with others? Our customers have the divine essence, too. Will we remember that people are covered in masks and conditioning, the kind that covers their brilliance? That we're all looking for an opportunity to unveil the greatness within? Who is willing to do what it takes to reveal the truth? To support one another?

Judgement is just a form of our conditioning. We use it for survival when we're young. We protect ourselves from the emotional turmoil, usually when we don't understand something. In judgement, we're in a state of object-referral, constantly seeking approval of others. We feel the need for external power, the need to control, which is fear-based, and our reference point is the ego.

When we're in a state of "self-referral," our reference point is internal, from our spiritual essence, immune to criticism, unfearful of any challenge, and beneath no one. Likewise, we're humble, and not superior to anyone. Self-power is creativity; it's true power. Ego power, which is competitive, can fall apart at any point. This is the concept of the Law of Pure Potentiality.

Why is this concept important to the Spirit of Selling? Just like separation is an illusion, competition with others is an illusion. Okay, right now I can hear you saying, "Are you crazy, Rhonda? Of course, there is competition!" Yes, there may be multiple suppliers for similar products and services, but what makes each one unique? You do.

Would you rather exist in an environment where you're at war every day? Do you want the stress of being under attack? Do you want to believe the pie is fixed, and that if you don't get your share, you'll starve? That you either win or lose?

Or would you prefer to believe that you can create opportunities, regardless of outside circumstances? That you can experience prosperity by developing your excellence? That the pie is infinite, and all you need to do is create more value?

For me, the second choice is much more appealing. It's easier to win with the mindset of a pro. I'll take calm confidence over stress any day. Self-mastery is freedom. It's unconditional love. Awareness is an infinite game. Always be humble.

Chapter VIII - Giving and Receiving is not the same as Getting and Taking

The Law of "Karma" or Cause and Effect, Sowing and Reaping, & The Law of Giving

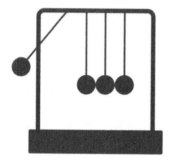

Get – to obtain; to come to have or hold.

Take – lay hold of with one's hand; to remove someone or something from a particular place.

Give – to freely transfer the possession of something to someone; to cause or allow to have; to provide or supply with.

Receive – to be given, presented with or paid.

"The Law of Cause and Effect is the Law of Laws" – Ralph Waldo Emerson

Nothing happens by chance or outside of Universal Law. Life, energy, and power operate in circulation, and you are life. Circulation means a continual flowing around. Spirit or infinite intelligence works in your world from the outside in through attraction, and from the inside out through action. Action is where the receiving happens and where the selling starts. On the cover of this book, you'll see a Fibonacci sequence. It's a symbol for the circulation of life.

Circulation is an infinite game, an investment for future return, an upward spiral. Think about your sales process through the principle of circulation, stewardship, and leaving the world better than you found it. When you adopt this philosophy, you can't lose. You're engaged in growth and expansion, which is infinite.

When you adopt a circulation principled sales mentality, you'll experience the bliss and ease of being in the spirit of selling. Why? Because you're working in harmony with Universal Law. I love the premise of the Law of Cause and Effect. When you truly understand it, you can't help but want to get busy giving. Understanding this law is knowing that whatever you put out will return, multiplied. What you shall sow, you will reap. And you always reap more than you sow. So easy, yet why do so many miss out on the concept?

Abraham Hicks gave a great explanation. Nonresistant thought is bliss. True bliss is complete harmony with who you are. But what causes you to resist bliss? You convinced yourself you are unworthy of it. Why? Because you think you need to calibrate to the others outside of you who suffer. The irony is humans calibrate themselves to their problems instead of their bliss.

When we got socialized and domesticated, we were told, "That's not the way life goes. Life is hard. Toughen up!" Consider accepting a new idea. The value you can be to others is contrast – evolution of species. It's easy to calibrate to what is on the outside. It takes mastery to calibrate to your dreams and be in complete alignment with who you are. Mastery takes an unwillingness to feel bad. It is as simple as this: feel good. When you are giving you feel good! Try that on.

The key question I ask my clients on a regular basis is, "Do you want to be the cause of your life, or the effect of it?" I love being the cause of my life – how about you? If you are looking for the law of life that will provide you peace of mind, and the time and money freedom you desire, this is the one to study, test, and apply to your life like a scientist.

To invest for a future return is completely different from a one-time trade. Investment indicates the possibility of a quantum leap, something infinite. A trade is finite. Newton's cradle is a great image to remind us of this principle. Energy is never lost; what you put out comes back. Put out a little effort, get a little back. Put out a lot of effort, get a lot back. Radiate positive energy, feel positive energy radiating back at you. Engage in negative energy and conditions, and watch the worry, doubt, and fear wreak havoc on your physical body.

There are no accidents. The Law of Cause and Effect, also known as the Law of Karma, is based on the scientific principle of a boomerang; chance is but a name we use when we have not yet recognized Law.

Think about it for a minute: action must be employed to manifest on the physical plane, and the same goes for manifesting sales. Every action you take creates momentum and produces an equal and opposite reaction. Karmic Law is becoming aware of the choices we make in every moment. Everything you are experiencing now is a result of the choices you made in the past, either consciously or unconsciously. There is another consequence to make note of. When you don't act, you put yourself in a position to be acted upon.

Our sales results never lie. Lack or abundance of sales are governed by either our use of universal law or our failure to use it. A good question to ask yourself is, "Am I working at the cause of my sales results or working with the effect of my sales results?" Remember, where your attention goes, the energy flows. You either *play the game and use the law* or you *become played in the game by others' wills and your environment.* I think it's easier to win when you decide to become the cause, to become conscious in the moment with your choices. Choose wisely, play the game, and take your power back.

Many salespeople are carried along. They respond to outside circumstances, or the wills, suggestion, and desires of people stronger than themselves. These outward causes move them like pawns on a chessboard. Their sales results are the effect of outside conditions—they give their power to the conditions: the economy, the recession, the competition, the pandemic, the reorganization, etc. Maybe they didn't consciously choose their job. Or they lost a job and quickly found another without thinking about a job they would love. They settle. They're on the hamster wheel of hurry, which is fear, and they can't seem to get off. They're stuck.

So, let's use the principle of cause and effect to explore some of the root causes for lack of sales results. Why aren't more salespeople winning? My answers go to belief in a finite power instead of an infinite power; ignorance of law; lack of skill; lack of confidence. There are more reasons, but these are the biggies. Let's dig deeper into these causes. How can you use this principle to take your power back and sell more?

Do you believe in a Finite Power or Infinite Power?

Beliefs are powerful. Beliefs that are defended, never questioned, can restrict, and stunt our results. Beliefs are cause, and results are effect. If we want to grow and expand, we must have an open mind. We must allow ourselves to entertain a few new ideas, especially if we don't like our results. Why is that? Because your existing beliefs will rob you of your dreams if your mind stays closed. So, before we move on, allow yourself this time to explore some new ideas. They say one idea can change your life forever.

The idea of access to infinite power was the one that changed my life. This was the one that finally set me free. I embraced it, tested it, and accepted it. In doing so, I released my fear of poverty forever and gained a peace and calmness of mind that is priceless. I tested the idea like a scientist for two solid years, applied it, and became fearless. If you have an open mind, and the willingness to evaluate a new idea, I'd like to share my story with you. Evaluate it, and determine if the idea of access to an infinite power would benefit you.

This may sound funny to you. I always thought God was out there, or up there—wherever Heaven was. I was on earth. I went to Catholic school and imagined God to be an old man with white hair, seated on a throne. Jesus was sitting on his right side, and all the saints were in this luxurious castle with them. I figured that when you die you float up there and meet St. Peter at the golden gate. St. Pete checks to see if you used your talents, and if you pass the test, you get to go in.

When you go in, you reconnect with all of your family and friends that passed away before you, unless they didn't get in. I always liked St Paul. I thought it would be cool to meet him because he was a great salesman. I used my imagination to comprehend what they taught us in religion class. Out of fear of missing out on the party, I've always been driven to unlock more of my potential, to do more, achieve more, and to play the endless game. I said prayers in church, but I certainly didn't rely on the power for everything.

I prayed when I was in trouble, but I never said prayers of gratitude when things were good. I figured God was busy with more important things and that I would do my best. I'd only go to him if I really needed something. I can't say I had any comprehension about being an instrument, a vessel to direct the power, except when we sang the Prayer of St Francis in church. My understanding was that of a child.

My concept of this power was finite. I thought I had to do it all myself. I had to generate the power. I was driven by achievement to the point of hyperachievement, the super woman complex, and I was exhausted. I didn't understand that I was a version of the same power; a Mini Me, like in the movie Austin Powers. My faith was about the size of a mustard seed, and I was in my fifties before I moved beyond that childlike awareness.

I read the Bible because I needed to understand a few things. In seeking, I found and began to understand that I had the power inside, not outside of me; that the kingdom of Heaven was within. This universal power wasn't confined to any one religion; it wasn't *out there*; it's everywhere, and everyone can use it, if you understand how to harmonize with it by *using* the law. Today I have adopted the mentality of the Queen. My life is easy, not hard, and I rely on the power for everything.

When you study, test, and apply what you learn, you'll understand the power is everything, and it does the work. We direct the power by fusing with it; I am the instrument, the vessel to direct it toward creation, and toward the expansion of life. Source energy is infinite. We project our beliefs on the universal power and mold it, either proactively with care, or by neglect. Energy is everywhere. It is indifferent, and it will give you anything. It's your choice as to how you want to direct it to cause.

But sometimes we trust it, and sometimes we don't. That's because we don't recognize our relationship with the power. The power is energy, and you are a ball of energy. You are made up of the same element: life. You are a center of distribution for life, connected and created in the image of the creator. The cool thing is that you get to decide on which version of that power you want to be. We talked about our unique gifts in the chapter on dharma, life's purpose. So, for simplicity's sake, suppose there are a million versions of life. The actual combinations of life are infinite.

When you show up on the planet with your dharma assignment, you get to pick from an infinite set of qualities and which ones you want to express. That choice is your personality; you set it by intention (dharma) and selection (choice). It is what makes you unique. That energy has universal laws, like the law of gravity. The energy can't change the law. The laws that apply to the universe also apply to you. Everything in harmony with the law continues to live, grow, and expand. It only gets blocked when we come up with new laws or beliefs that aren't in harmony with universal source energy.

When we think we can't get what we want, we project fear on source energy. The power becomes finite because of the environment of the vessel it's in—you're the vessel. We constrict and stunt our vessel. Remember, we are the instrument. The only limiting beliefs we have are self-imposed. The cause is the limitation we put on ourselves with belief—or lack of belief.

In 2019, my position was eliminated and my belief busting journey began. I made the decision to start a business from scratch, and I focused on what I could give. I looked up volunteer opportunities and found one: gardening at the historical center. I signed up to be a CCD teacher at the church; I volunteered to give group coaching lessons at the Women's Center. I made monthly visits to my parents and helped my dad to get his book published. I did free master classes for my coaching business, and live social media posts on positivity.

On the financial investment side, I decided to invest in myself, my business, my home, and my family relationships. This is where I busted all my money beliefs and applied the Law of Circulation. The old belief was, "You can't touch your 401k money until you are 59.5 years old. You'll get whacked with tax penalties." That was extremely limiting. All my equity was tied up in the stock market. I had put two kids through college over a six-year period. My home needed renovations, but they were put on hold. I needed money to invest in my business, and I was tired of stay-cations and weekend beach trips.

But that old belief wasn't true! I heard about the rule of 55. I investigated and found that 401k income from the employer I left involuntarily could be regular income. I had another 401k account that was not converted, and any company stock I owned had a tax advantage for one time at point of transfer. The story kept getting better, and the belief was busted.

My next move was to test the "investment" principle. When I began to invest and got the money circulating, it multiplied! I invested $30,000 in a family trip to Europe. It was absolutely amazing! I invested another $50K in my business. I invested more than $300k in my home. It was completely updated. Now I live in opulent surroundings, and it feels amazing to have everything clean, new, and orderly. I'm not trying to impress you. I'm telling you this to impress *upon you* that if it worked for me, and it can work for you.

I became a believer when I calculated my net worth in 2021 and compared it to my net worth in 2019. I gave it away, provided jobs and work for multiple people, and it all came back! My earning potential has increased exponentially. I discovered how to develop multiple streams of income. Instead of two streams of income, I now have five. Am I happy that I challenged my beliefs and tested the power? You bet I am!

If you drift and think the power is outside of you, something you have no influence on, you'll lose and be played in the game; you will be at the effect of your results. Anything outside of you that has power in your life only exists because you give it that power. For example, money doesn't give you security; infinite power gives you security. You don't get paid by your employer; you get paid through your employer. The tomato plant doesn't come from the seed, it comes through the seed. The sale doesn't come from the prospect, it comes through the prospect. Everything circulates.

The secret is pushing the limits of action. Why? Because energy must be released. So, if you want to sell more, all you have to do is give more! You have many gifts to give, not just your time. Passion, compassion, empathy, listening, affection, attention, acknowledgement, appreciation, love, creativity, time, and money. This is the secret that I uncovered in my fifties and alluded to during my book launch. You have divinity within you; it's your higher self, your sage, your spiritual DNA. It's love— your passion and compassion.

Your sage knows that you have the ability to fuse with an infinite power, to create and direct that power to serve others in harmony while living in opulence. If you don't feel free, ask yourself, "Where am I constricting the power? And why?" Your sage knows we are all connected by this power; we operate like one body. Every person has his or her own gift to share with the body. There are many parts to the human body: a liver provides detox services, while the heart oxygenates the blood, the lungs regulate the breathing, and the eyes provide vision.

You and I have unique divine qualities to be shared and given to the world. Our source of supply is infinite when we are in alignment with law, growing and expanding. The abundance is the result of application of the law: the power source is infinite. It works just like electricity. Put a 40-watt light bulb in the socket, and the light emitted is 40 watts; insert a 1000-watt bulb, the light emitted is 1000 watts. The energy expands as a function of the vessel it is applied in. If your vessel is constricting the flow in any way, the infinite power becomes finite. You choose.

Life grows and expands through the process of circulation, giving and receiving. But most of us forget that. Why? During our domestication process, we activated our saboteur, the judge who became more prevalent than our true self, our sage. Fear is used to control. Here's the problem: fear turns infinite power to finite power. Fear is the belief that you can't get what you want. Fear is how you became domesticated; its why you become attached to things, and it's what causes you struggle.

Fear is when you have no desire, no imagination, and no confidence. Source is free of resistance. Infinite power lies within us, but we reduce it with our conscious mind. Your thinking is controlling your life. Want more? Change your thinking, and evaluate your beliefs. Surround yourself with people who have accomplished what you want. Do what you love!

When we learn to rely on an infinite source with faith, we operate in bliss and ease. When we learn to feed our desires and starve our fears by controlling what we think about, we release resistance. Faith is knowing; love is feeling and knowing. Knowing is awareness of law.

Ignorance of Law & lack of skill. The common misconception for salespeople is to give with an intention to get. I get it. I've been there too. You need cash, and you're giving, but it's not happening fast enough. It's frustrating. Eighty percent of your communication is non-verbal, and people can sense when you need them more than they need you. It comes across; they feel it. It's a turn off for new prospects. If you understand the Law of Circulation, you won't expect to receive from everyone you give to because you know selling is not trading; it's investing, always leaving the other person with an impression of increase.

You'll concentrate on serving the other, knowing that by law it will come back. The Law of Circulation states, "*To whom you give is not necessarily from whom you will receive.*" The secret to "getting" is giving. And the secret to giving is making yourself open to receiving. The Law of Receptivity is a bit of a paradox. Inside every truth and every appearance, there is a bit of the opposite.

If life requires circulation, then it's important that we understand the difference between trading (get and take) and circulating (giving and receiving). Get and take are finite concepts. Give and receive are investments you pay forward. Those investments cause life to spiral up, to expand for greater expression. Life expands infinitely through the circulation system of giving and receiving.

But some of us accept the idea that it's better to give than to receive. So, let's debunk that one right here and now. If you believe that, you're blocking sales. That idea is as ridiculous as believing it's better to exhale than to inhale. Or the idea that it's better for your heart to relax than contract.

It's insane to try to give and not receive. Receiving is the natural result of giving. All the giving in the world won't make you successful, not unless you're willing to receive in like measure! When you refuse to receive, you shut down the flow in the circulation system. You block it and send it elsewhere. If you had a block like that in your heart, your life would stop. The laws of nature apply to sales. Keep everything circulating. Want more, give more, and be willing to graciously receive.

If you haven't thought about it before, there are two forms of income: psychic and material. The psychic income comes from the fulfillment of doing something you love and sharing it with someone else. The material income comes from expectation, and fulfilling the Law of Compensation, which is a secondary Law of Cause and Effect. The Law of Compensation states you will be paid based upon the need for what you do, your ability to do it, and the difficulty in replacing you. Your ability to do your work, to enhance your skill, is the cause and effect of your sales results; it's the part you control.

Action is where the receiving happens. Give yourself the gift of investing in you. How often do you simulate and practice your sales process? Do you write it out? Are you clear on what you're selling and what outcomes you'll provide for your clients? Do you always ask yourself, after every call, what did I do well? What can I do better? What did I learn from this experience that I can leverage for my next client? How can I improve my service? How can I leave everyone with an impression of increase, whether they buy or not? The better you become at serving others, the more sales you'll make.

Confidence If you lack confidence, be honest and ask yourself, "What, if anything, have I been procrastinating on?" Practicing your presentation? Contacting people? Following up with someone? Making sales calls? Deciding? And why? Are you in a habit of asking everyone for their opinions? How often do you ask yourself what to do? Think hard about that one. The root of any confidence problem lies in procrastination. The opposite of procrastination is decision. Procrastinators lack action; no action, no results. They lack confidence because they're not making decisions. Making decisions has only one pre-requisite: do you want it?

The more decisions you make, the more confidence you gain. If you want to be the cause of your life, you set the direction for your life and direct your power. You direct your power by making decisions. The better you are at making decisions, the more effective you'll be at persuading your customers to make decisions. If you don't make decisions, you'll be acted upon.

Remember the boomerang? You can't give what you don't have. Think about your recent sales calls. When it comes to having your customers decide, are you confident that you'll help them make that decision? Rate yourself on a scale of 1 to 10. How confident are you in their decision? Do you visualize the sale before the call starts?

If you wring your hands and worry about what others think, and if you seek ten opinions before you decide, you'll attract prospects just like you. You'll let your customers off the hook, just like you let yourself off the hook. Make more decisions consciously, on your own. Watch your confidence soar, and observe the rise of your customers' confidence in you. More decisions, more confidence, more sales. Make sense?

If you dig deeper and ask what causes procrastination, you'll realize that the governor in your subconscious mind, your self-image, is stopping you. I see this happen all the time when people transition to new roles. It can happen during promotions, the transition to a new company, a new sales arena, or during a move from salary to commission. If the governor isn't updated, and the reset button isn't activated, you'll suffer from imposter syndrome. You need to feel worthy of becoming the person you want to become. Learn how to quiet your saboteur judge and build your self-command muscle. Unleash your sage. The divinity within you is the path to your freedom and confidence. For more on the self-image, refer back to chapter VI, *Sell Yourself on You.*

Champions, the masters at selling, know that higher planes of thinking dominate the lower. To be movers instead of pawns on a chess board, they must dominate and control moods, actions, character, and environment. They choose to obey and use the principle instead of being the tool or the mechanics for the principle. Are you actively deciding to be the cause or the effect of your life? And your sales results? Are you consciously making decisions that are in harmony with the law?

The law of Karma suggests three steps to enhance your decisions. First, be fully conscious in the present moment. Use your will to stay in the now. Second, ask yourself some questions. "What are the consequences of this choice I am making?" and "Will this choice bring fulfillment and happiness to me? Who is affected by this choice?" Ask your heart for guidance by its message of comfort or discomfort. If you feel comfortable, charge ahead. If you feel uncomfortable, pause, and see the consequences of your action with your inner vision. Listen to your heart.

Chapter IX – Get into the Flow and Ride the Surf!

The Law of Rhythm and the Law of Polarity

"Happiness is not a matter of intensity but of balance, order, rhythm, and harmony." – Thomas Merton

"He who lives in harmony with himself, lives in harmony with the universe." – Marcus Aurelius

Have you ever heard the saying, "Don't die with your music left in you?" Or "Let your heart sing?" The inference is that we all have potential to create more music and harmony through our heart power. It is the harnessing of that heart power potential that places you on a trajectory for quantum leaps. It's the secret to happiness. Start applying these laws to selling and watch your sales results skyrocket!

Did you know that your heart has an electromagnetic field that is five-thousand times stronger than the brain's? The heart's magnetic field is the strongest *rhythmic* field produced by the body. It resonates in the cells and extends into the space that surrounds it. Sammy Davis Jr. sang a song a long time ago called "The Rhythm of Life," in the movie *Sweet Charity*. The refrain in the song said, "The rhythm of life is a powerful beat!" Science has proven it is! Balance, harmony, and music in your heart makes life more enjoyable.

This chapter is all about balance and rhythm that produce harmony. The two laws that help us regulate our heart power and our emotional mind are the Law of Polarity and the Law of Rhythm. They work synergistically together. The Law of Polarity is all about balance and duality, while the Law of Rhythm is about the speed of the pendulum.

Nature has seasons and cycles, and so do your sales results. Those seasons give us rhythm and balance. Jim Rohn compared sales cycles to the seasons. He would say, "You can't have two springs and eliminate the winter." In the spring you cultivate the soil and sow seeds. It's a short season so seize the opportunity! In the summer you nourish, protect and defend the crops in the garden. This is the high drama season where you behold the possibilities and the dangers; in the fall you reap the harvest. Life gives you what you deserve, not what you need. In the winter, you reflect and prepare for the next season.

Life is not linear, it has rhythm, contrast, pitch, dynamics, and duration. That's what provides the adventure and fulfillment. Those who learn to adapt themselves to the flow outside, and radiate an internal harmonious rhythm inside, become a surfer of the waves, and those people thrive. Those who lack the understanding, who resist the flow, and lack internal harmony, will experience some pain, some bumps and bruises from being at the effect of their outside conditions and circumstances.

What are your sales cycles like? Do you experience big swings in your sales results? Peaks and valleys? Have you found the secret to creating harmonious momentum and rhythm in your work? Do you expect that if you blow out your plan this year, next year will be bleak or tough? Or do you expect more success every year and feel unlimited in your potential? When you are in a downswing, do you wait for the other shoe to drop or expect that you are about to climb up a new higher mountain? When something doesn't work out as you planned, do you see it as negative? Or do you look for the good, the gift in it?

I ask these questions to get you to start thinking about your mindset. Do you tend to perceive your life and situations on a radio preset? Are you always looking at life through the same rose-colored glasses, or do you try on various glasses to enrich your perspective? Are you on autopilot with your assumptions? In other words, do you think just because it happened before it will happen again? Or do you actively choose positive assumptions or meanings?

Are you bringing past sales scenarios into your new year? If so, are they positive or negative? Do they serve you? Or do you operate in curiosity, on the manual method of adjusting your radio station daily in the now? These questions are important because they influence your commissions and your sales results.

Let's start by discussing the *cause* of the ebbs and flows we experience. We become what we think about. It all starts with a vibration becoming a thought. When you pick up a thought, you translate the vibration with your emotions. You have a vibrational translator within you, your heart, and it speaks to you. How aware are you of your emotions? Do you listen to them or dismiss them? What is an emotion anyway?

My interpretation, after reading Michael Singer's book, *The Untethered Soul*, is that emotion is energy passing through the heart and before the eye of consciousness. I sit in the seat of my awareness, like watching a movie in a movie theatre. I feel and observe the emotion, and it gives me feedback about the direction I am moving in. I either release the emotion or hold onto it. I either contract my heart and close it in resistance, or I relax and open my heart, feel the emotion to get the translation, and release the emotion. That is the difference in polarity, the choice we get to make, to close or release energy through our heart. We were made to release energy. When you listen to your heart, your higher self is speaking to you with wisdom. The more open the heart, the more energy flows through it.

Let's remember cause, a vibration transformed into thought. We translated that thought by feeling an emotion. We either let the emotion pass and received the feedback, or we closed our heart to resist feeling it.

When you hear someone say, "They made me so mad!" or "Boy, Jack really pushed Jill's buttons," you are observing the contracting and closing of one's heart and a display of ignorance. The ignorance stems from lack of an individual's awareness that the control switch to choose their emotions and feelings is within. We have the power to choose. The outside world does not have power to give us a translation. What we feel is a choice. But if you are on autopilot, not consciously choosing in the now what you want to feel, or assuming someone or something is doing it to you, you give your power away.

People can't push your buttons unless you allow their actions to affect you. Awareness allows you to become responsible for your emotions by activating your responsibility powers, your response-ability. You can respond by taking your power back and observing the message. Understand the music. If it feels good, you are happy, connected with source, and going in the right direction. You will be like Gru in *Despicable Me 2*, dancing to the "Happy" Song! If it feels bad, you are going in the wrong direction. Observe the translation, and decide which direction you want to move in. If the feeling serves you, hold onto it, if not discard it. Stay focused on what you want.

Many of our emotions stem from values, beliefs, and assumptions which are active vibrations of thought, not thought from the past, but in the present. Most of our beliefs are inherited from our genetic and environmental conditioning; we do not choose them. You accepted those beliefs as a child to support your security. Remember Linus in Peanuts, and his security blanket? Many of the beliefs you hold onto are like a security blanket. Someone else gave those thoughts to you, you accepted them to be truth, and you keep them activated.

Those beliefs have a governor's voice attached to them. That governor is your inner critic, your saboteur. Think of your conditioning, your current beliefs, as your software version from the domestication process. Conditioning is a form of control with conditional love and attachments, like Linus' security blanket. I'm not saying some beliefs don't serve you well. But allow yourself to reevaluate them, especially if you're stuck. If your sales suffer from approval addiction, that's stemming from your domestication. Too often people are unconscious of their beliefs and how they close their minds to new ideas.

Our awareness and development outpace the old programing, and the old thoughts are in conflict with new vibrations. And as a result, many people settle in conformity, thinking this is as good as it gets. If you're not consciously aware of those beliefs, the paradigms you have, they will stay in charge of you, keeping you right where you are, bumping up against a glass ceiling. The only way to bust through is to get a software update so your beliefs can catch up with your awareness.

The easiest way to mitigate that governor conflict is to stop thought and stop the resistance, so you can hear and gain direction from your ally, your sage, to support you. That's why meditation is beneficial. You let those thoughts go, get out of the drama of the movie, and get back into your observer's seat. When the resistant beliefs are suspended, they are not in the way of what your inner being, your essence knows and is trying to tell you. When you quiet the mind, you let your evolution show itself to you; you allow your vibration to rise and can feel your intuition communicate to you.

The other way to reprogram yourself with a new belief, one that matches your new desire, is through autosuggestion. Working with a coach puts you on a fast track to adopting new beliefs because the coach will hold the belief for you until yours kicks in. Suggestion is the most powerful force in the world.

Why bother doing this? To realize your desires and experience them!

The Law of Rhythm dictates we need to balance our desire, an emotionalized want, with our belief (the compensator) to contour our expectations to let what we want come into our lives. We need harmony and unity between our desires and beliefs. The problem we all face as humans is that we want something, then we doubt we can have it because it has not yet appeared in our garage. We get annoyed with the lag time; there is no balance (polarity) in our attraction.

Know this: the minute you ask for something, source energy is bringing it to you. Remember the Sermon on the Mount? Ask and it shall be given to you? Desire and belief are both emotions. You want them to be in harmony so you can receive the good you desire. Desire summons the process. Belief and expectation are the rhythm emotions to compensate the opening for you to receive what you desire.

The number one problem that stops manifestation is disbelief. By focusing on the "ISN'T-NESS" you are putting up a shield that blocks the good that you desire. Belief or "IS-NESS" opens. The negative emotion of disbelief cancels out desire. To orchestrate your music and attract what you want in your life, your job is to FEEL it, believing it is here, act as if it's done. Then LET, allow your desire to unfold before you and enjoy the process.

A belief or assumption is nothing more than an idea you accept to be true. So, for goodness' sake, open your mind and allow yourself to check your programming, and re-evaluate your beliefs and assumptions. If they are not serving you, empowering you to go after your dreams, blow them up! Columbus decided he wasn't buying the idea that the world was flat. The Wright brothers were not going to buy into the idea that it was impossible to fly. Let's wake up!

One way to re-evaluate your assumptions and beliefs is to look at their polarity. This is where you can use the Law to your advantage. During the pandemic I ran some master classes on "Brave Thinking." You can watch the webinar on my website, www.3x5coaching.com/webinar/. In the webinar I discuss the polarity of assumptions and the four "R 's" to develop the resilience of a diamond in times when your personal control will not alter outside circumstances and waves. This is the path of least resistance.

The four R's are strategies that activate more of your heart power. **Release** and let go is step number one. We were made to release energy, not to suppress or restrict it. When the heart holds on to a thorn, a thought that produces emotional pain, it suffers. It's better to let the thorn go and heal. Learn from it. Release it.

Relief means to give up the attachment, to unchain yourself from it. Be free like a butterfly and touch everything lightly. Nothing in life is permanent. You are passing through life, and when you leave you won't take anything with you. Everything is moving, so enjoy the encounter by observing it with awe and curiosity. Be detached. Watch the movie.

Reflect is taking your attention and directing it towards the good, the positive pole, and asking, what's the gift in this for me? Duality is everywhere. Be curious. And forgive the rest. To forgive is for your benefit.

Last, **Redirect** your attention toward a new intention for good. Focus, using the Law of Polarity. Set an intention, remembering that the bigger the adversity, the bigger the gift because the Law of Rhythm compensates. Create new possibility and allow yourself to be open to it. Those four qualities enable the emergence of your resilience.

To assume is to think something without any proof. There are dangers and wins on both ends of the spectrum of assumption. Selling is a partnership of trust between you and the client. Most salespeople are overly optimistic. Depending upon the degree of optimism, you could have "happy ears," which means you hear what you want to hear or you rely on hope. But hope is not a strategy. When you're engaged in a partnership or connection with a client, your assumptions should in alignment with the customer's view of their promised land, not yours.

You must have some elements of objective reality, a balanced perspective with the client. Your instrument or service is not what your customer will buy. They are buying their vision, an idea of a new promised land—project completion, confidence, security, or whatever else they want. Your job is to turn their want into a desire. No desire, no sale. When they feel your alignment, they will begin to know, like, and trust you. This is when you will be able to suggest and persuade to sell for them instead of to them.

You either use the power of assumption or become used by it. Assumption is more common in your life than you might realize. Assumptions that are positive cause you to *express* yourself. Negative assumptions cause you to *suppress* yourself. Nature operates on expansion of expression. To gain alignment with nature, source energy, the flow, focus on assumptions that allow for your expansion.

Check your mindset. When a client cancels an appointment, what is the first thought that runs through your mind? Do you assume they are not interested, or do you assume something must have come up and they can't wait to reschedule? When a customer says *I need a new car*, do you think you have an order because you sell cars and asked a question? Or do you realize you will need to ask many more questions to understand what the customer wants, where they are, where they want to be, what else they are looking for, what their motives are, who are they are evaluating besides you, and if they have funding?

If you are not getting the sales results you want, ask yourself, "Is my mindset focused on the Negative pole or the Positive pole of this situation?" If you find you are on the negative pole, ask yourself, "What would I need to notice, appreciate, or believe to change the outcome and shift my focus?

Question number two is, "Is my perception of this problem on auto-pilot? If I write the problem on paper and put the paper on the table is the problem in me, my perception, or on the paper? Am I being present in the now? If you are in the now, you will always validate where you are starting from. This is objective reality, being honest with yourself. What information do I know, what do I need to know or confirm? What's missing? Where can I go to find the answer and validate truth?

Most companies and businesses look to shorten sales cycles and predict trends. You help your company by uncovering truth. Commonplace is to look at past trends to predict future ones. These are linear strategies because they use the past to predict future. They serve a purpose, but Champions who want to experience non-linear results look at heart of the matter, your true power source.

The Law of Polarity and the Law of Rhythm regulate the speed and degree of swing in your sales cycles. They allow you to adjust and to control your destiny. You build momentum and create more music and harmony on the journey. You expand and grow your business in a state of happiness. Your heart is aligned with these laws, and what's in your heart is controlling your actions, which control your results. If you'd like to be at the cause of your results, orchestrate the music inside you to attract more of what you want. Ride the waves.

The Law of polarity states that everything is dual; that pairs of opposites may be reconciled, that opposites are identical in their nature, but different in degree. The exciting part of this principle is that everything in life has duality! Polarity is oneness. It is connected, not absolute. And there is always a positive pole in every situation, no matter what the circumstance. This is key to understand.

Think of one long pole. One end has a positive charge, the other a negative charge. Think of one cell in your body. One end has an apical membrane, the other a basal membrane. The duality helps us to appreciate both ends of the pole, the oneness of it, what one end does and feels like versus the other. It's the contrast that helps us choose. It allows one to appreciate and feel grateful for what is present, what is good. It raises awareness.

The ancient symbol of harmony, the yin and the yang circle, reminds us that life is a balancing act and most fulfilling when we learn to embrace its dualities instead of resisting them; the ups and downs, the flow and inflow, the ebb and tide, the good times and the bad, the joys and the challenges. Balance leads to happiness. For example, there is no place on a thermometer where heat ceases and cold begins. The higher of two degrees is always "warmer" while the lower one is "colder." Good and bad are not absolute, they are just two ends of the same pole. Both are present, the question is which one do you look for and focus on? The same is true on the mental plane with our emotions. There are no absolutes, just opposites that vary by degree.

Peggy McColl wrote an amazing book called, *Your Destiny Switch*, in which she uses the analogy of a dimmer switch to explain how you can control and adjust your emotions. She explains that emotions are fractures of light, like a prism. The dimmer switch is one switch with two poles representing its duality. The cool thing about the switch analogy is that it reminds us of where the power is. You have the power to adjust the light switch where you want it, to control the direction of the source energy and the ambiance of your environment.

Some examples of emotion polarities or opposites include love and hate, wonder and emptiness, bliss and depression, faith and worry; rage and calm, abundance and poverty; decision and procrastination; confidence and insecurity, ignorance and understanding, inspiration and discouragement.

Remember how strong the heart power is? Where your attention goes, your energy flows. You can start using your heart power to work for you to sell more. Emotions can use you, or you can use them. To be at the cause of your results, start listening to your emotions. Don't shove those emotions under a rug. Your heart is trying to communicate with you. When your heart is open, you gain wisdom. A choice to contract is to separate. A choice to open is to join. The tendency of nature is always in the direction of harmony and the dominant activity of the positive pole. You can't be on the positive and negative pole at the same time. Let's hold that thought, and ask this question. "What would I need to notice, appreciate, or believe to move in the direction of the dominant positive pole?" Next, let's relate polarity to the word *spirit* to see where you are on the "spirit meter." Spirit is life, connected to source, expansion, and greater expression. The opposite of life is death, suppression, constriction, separation from source.

Spirit is love; hate is on the opposite pole.

Spirit is light; the opposite pole is darkness.

Spirit is power; the opposite pole is force.

Spirit is peace; the opposite pole is conflict.

Spirit is beauty; the opposite pole is ugliness.

Spirit is joy and bliss; the opposite pole is depression.

If you're not producing the sales results you desire, try out this exercise using the law of polarity. Get a piece of paper and fold it in half. Describe what you're assuming about your current situation. Place all your current assumptions on the left side of the page and mark them as positive or negative. On the right side of the page, write the exact opposite. Go through the list and circle the ones you want. Ask yourself some additional questions:

- What do I assume failure to be?

- What intent do I want to assume?

- How can I stay in the day and leave the past in the past?

- Are there any *contracting* assumptions I can replace with *connective* assumptions?

- How can I assume the wish fulfilled? What would I need to notice, appreciate, or believe to alter my assumption?

- Do all my assumptions empower me?

- Am I willing to shift my focus to "how I can" vs "why I can't"?

Next, apply the synchronicity of the Law of Rhythm. The Law of Rhythm states that everything flows, out and in; everything rises and falls; the pendulum swing manifests in everything. Life is a balancing act and rhythm compensates. Rhythm is the measured motion between the two poles of the positive and negative. The motion is the measured speed of the swing back and forth. The strongest rhythmic field in your body is your heart. So, fall in love with what you are doing; remember your why.

Picture your sales process as one pole. On the left end is the stage where you identify your prospects for your sales funnel and begin to develop rapport and trust. On the right end is the number of clients who said yes. Your sales presentation and follow up are in between the initial contact and the close. There is a certain rate of speed for that funnel. Many refer to it as funnel velocity. How quickly do you move your prospects through the funnel, and how many new prospects can you gain over a fixed period of time? If you are not getting the results you want, you can apply the Law of Rhythm to your sales process.

The Law of Compensation is rhythm. We talked about the Law of Compensation in an earlier chapter. Your compensation is dependent upon the quality of your product or service, and the quantity of people it impacts. Three factors impact your compensation: the demand for what you do, your ability to sell, and the difficulty in replacing you. We are told to focus on our ability to sell and the rest will take care of itself. But we need a system: perfect your sales presentation; fire up your desires; improve your self-image and confidence and develop empowering habits. These things impact your compensation.

Our sales rhythm impacts energy and action. The greater the buy-in and motivation observed, the less tension and anxiety exists, and the speed of vibration increases towards the positive pole. The swings are not wide. The distance between the peaks and valleys decreases, and the rhythm becomes consistent and controlled, but only if you are using the law. Increased action means increased return.

Ask yourself, how much rhythm do you have in your sales process? Is it systematized? Bullet proof? Smooth? Like harmonious music? Is it running as smooth as a symphony, or does it sound like an amateur band? Are you closing sales consistently? In the flow of ease and bliss? If not, it's time to get yourself into a rhythm. Rhythm causes the music in our life. Movement takes part in rhythm. Movement means action.

Focus, physiology, and tonality impact rhythm as well. Harmonious rhythm builds momentum. And all momentum starts with some resistance to get it off the ground. Momentum in the case of selling is habits. Harmony is based in cooperation and consistency. Order gains orders.

Here is where mindset comes in. I believe selling is 95% mindset and 5% mechanics. If you are going to sell by law and not by luck, you must master your "response-ability." Your mindset is regulating your heart power. An open heart allows source energy to flow. And when you develop a positive mental mindset, you are likely to develop a "Pleasing Personality" and will learn to "Polarize" your mind toward the positive. The game is to go positive for a minimum of 51% of the time.

When you learn to polarize your own mind, you learn that mental induction is possible, and you can use it to persuade others. You become the orchestra director of that electromagnetic power source. Suggestion is the most powerful force in the world. You may want to underline or highlight that statement because it is important, and it is true. Mental Induction works like a magnet, or electricity, or a sound wave. It's cause and effect: what you put out, comes back.

By becoming the master of your mental state instead of the servant and slave to your judge, your saboteur, and your circumstances, you can aid your fellows intelligently and change the polarity of those around you. This understanding will throw light on many difficult subjects or personalities. It's easier to win when we shift from being a controller of outside circumstances to a curious surfer, aligned with law and harmony, touching lightly, and riding the waves. You can't control wind and waves, but you can be an awesome surfer!

How? You apply your sage perspective; you ask, "How can I view and apply this situation as a gift to feel flow and joy instead of pain and punches?" Here's an example of the sage vs the saboteur perspective. In March 2020, we experienced the beginning of a pandemic. Most people were working remotely. During that time, I interviewed multiple Sales Directors and small business owners. How were their teams adjusting to the new conditions for selling? I found polarity in the responses.

Some sales organizations were stagnant. It was near impossible to get appointments and new clients. I asked what they thought was holding them back. The answer I received from some was that no one was willing to do Zoom calls; no one had funding, and live in-person calls were necessary to uncover needs. They were downsizing. Yet other organizations were experiencing record sales in 2020, finishing the year twenty to fifty percent over plan and adding people. When I asked why they were so successful, they were confident in their product, what problems it could solve, and they found they could have more sales presentations in a day via virtual meetings. They did more in less time. Their productivity and rhythm were increasing.

Here's the paradox. The masters fixate themselves on the desired state; they focus on the positive and leverage it to their advantage. They are not attached to the old ways and mechanics. Their mastery allows them to neutralize circumstance and experience relief by detachment from the old. They apply curiosity to the new circumstance and redirect their energy to uncover the gift: what's in it for them to rise above the situation. In contrast, those who are attached to the old way of doing things, those unwilling to release and let go, contract, suppress and experience decline and separation.

It's not as simple as positive thinking. It requires honest thinking and allowing yourself the ability to examine your beliefs, values, and assumptions. Update your programming.

Your beliefs, assumptions, attitudes, and perceptions are causing your life. You will never go beyond what you believe you are. Belief is nothing more than an idea you accept to be true. If your beliefs are not empowering you, they are not truth.

Be willing to be a belief buster and to choose positive assumptions. Take your power back and consciously choose your beliefs. Get your belief in harmony with your desires. The polarity control switch of your heart is inside you; it's not out there. Keep your heart open and let the energy flow. Remember, rhythm compensates, it releases energy, your music. Every outcome can be turned into a gift. Don't die with your music left inside. Let your heart sing!

Chapter X – Allow You and Your Gifts to Bloom

The Law of Gestation & The Law of Pure Potentiality

"As a Man thinketh in his heart, so is he." – Proverbs 23:7

"You will know them by their fruits."- Matthew 7, 15-20

"Do not repay anyone evil for evil. Be careful to do what is right in the eyes of everyone. "-Romans 12:17

     Have you ever played in the dirt? Perhaps you have a flower or vegetable garden. Or as a child, maybe you planted sunflowers in the back yard and watched them grow? I'm going to tell you about a universal law that will revolutionize your business and your sales results. It is not the Law of Attraction, but it activates the Law of Attraction. It's called the Law of Gestation. I love it because you can use the images of the gardening process on the physical plane to relate to an invisible concept in your mind. When you start applying this "gardener mindset" to your business and your sales processes, magic happens.

A gestation period is defined as the time between conception and birth. For example, human babies have an average gestation period of forty weeks. A tomato can take anywhere from 45-100 days to produce fruit. All life has a gestation period, including your sales. Creation requires elements of gender, masculine and feminine energy, to produce results. You are here in physical form because of mom and dad, who created you. You must have a female and male holly bush to produce the red berries. Keep those thoughts handy as we dig deeper into this law.

Everything in life is created twice, first by a concept in the mind, then by its manifestation. All concepts start in the imagination. Think of your imagination as your workshop for conception, your playground for creation. Perhaps you are in a new sales position, and you can imagine yourself being named rookie of the year at the annual sales meeting. Or you believe this is the year you will earn the inner circle award. Maybe you like to imagine six or seven figure commissions?

Napoleon Hill said, "The Imagination is the most marvelous, miraculous, inconceivably powerful force in the world." When you go to your imagination, you can experience reality there, as clearly as on the physical plane. In the imagination you can feel things. You can experience emotions. There is a place. And the feelings are where conception begins. Andrew Carnegie said, "Any *idea* that is held in the mind that is either *feared or revered* will, begin at once to clothe itself in the most convenient and appropriate physical forms available." All gardeners know that anything they can imagine first in their mind, they can create in their garden. By applying the cardinal rules of gardening to your sales process, you can do the same!

The Wright Brothers had an idea they fell in love with: they wanted to fly. I am certain those ideas were first generated in their imagination. Walt Disney fell in love with an idea of entertainment through cartoons, like Mickey Mouse. Mickey was a character Walt first met in his imagination. All manifestations start with an idea. The idea is a seed, a patterned plan in the mind. When it gets planted, it becomes a conception, the beginning of life. The seeds sown in the garden bloom. The manifestation of that idea is its birth. Birth is the effect, the reaping, the condition created.

The imagination is unconditional. Anything can be planted in there. The difference between the pros and the amateur salesperson is that the pros take full control over that imagination and purposely plant what they want. If you are not getting the sales results you desire, you have not yet mastered full control over your garden.

Gestation is the space between the creation of a concept and its manifestation. When you accept and get in flow with The Law of Gestation, you can enjoy the process. Too often we see impatience with sales results. I am talking about the impatience that is fear driven from hurry instead of faith driven from urgency. I imagine this is due to ignorance of nature's laws for gardening. The good news is that by understanding this law, the benefits of urgency and faith, that there always will be a gestation period, that you can always be sowing. But you do not reap and sow in the same season. You can appreciate and enjoy the journey unconditionally with calm and ease.

Watching things grow and bloom and partaking in the process can teach us so many things about how to sell, and about ourselves. Proverbs 23:7 isn't talking about the muscle in your chest. The heart there is the mind-body connection: your emotional mind, your garden, your playground for creation, and your physical heart that generates your body's vibrational frequency. More than 96% of your human potential and inner power is in your emotional subconscious mind. But very few people really understand how the mind is the instrument through which source energy flows. Whatever is planted in the garden of your mind creates your results.

In the last chapter we talked about the electromagnetic field of your heart being 5000 times greater than the field of logic. This electromagnetic field is like a plot of land. It belongs to you. Only you can plant in it. That is, unless you give that power away. Source energy runs through that land. Source energy is like a magnet and is very powerful when it is channeled or magnetized, meaning all the electrons are ordered in one clear direction. The energy field of the magnet is always present.

However, that energy field can become demagnetized if its electrons are out of order. The electrons in your heart center plot of land are your thoughts. Do you believe your heart center is magnetized, or has it become demagnetized? Are your thoughts ordered or all over the place? Do you suffer from FOMO (fear of missing out), or shiny object syndrome, constantly distracted by outside circumstances? Or are you resolute and focused on your mission, like a Navy Seal? If you want to amplify the magnetism in your mind, just create some order in your garden. Activate that power and put it to use.

I want you to think like a gardener. Your sales and the growth of your business start with concepts, a goal, or a seed. These are the ideas you fall in love with. That concept, goal, or seed will manifest based upon a gestation period if it's successfully planted in the garden of your mind. Birth and creation require the elements of masculine and feminine energy. That is law. But not everyone understands how to plant, how to use both the male and female energy to create; so, let's get some basic gardening lessons addressed.

Joseph Murray, in his book *The Power of your Subconscious Mind,* describes your mind as having two parts, the masculine and feminine. Your conscious mind, the thinking mind, is the masculine energy that thinks, creates, and formulates ideas from thoughts; it's the part of your mind that sets goals. It is action focused. Your subconscious or emotional mind is the feminine energy, the soil where you plant thought seeds for your dreams and desires, your electromagnetic field and power center. This garden soil bears the traits of reflection; what you put in; you get back.

The characteristics of your emotional mind are re-evaluation and course correction, meaning it is a cybernetic instrument to ensure you stay in alignment with your destination, and it serves as an auto-pilot function that course corrects. It is the place where all your habits, beliefs, and perceptions reside with your self-image. It's the part of your mind that drives your behavior and your results. It is where you store all the things you accept as truth. These accepted thoughts are your assumptions. The garden of your mind accepts what you give it. Our results outside are always a reflection of what is going on inside.

Is there a difference between birth on the physical plane and birth on the spiritual plane? Yes. Your desires, the longing or dissatisfaction you experience, are spiritual seeds. The methods for creation from the spiritual plane differ from the methods used to create on the mental plane. You know a thing mentally by the appearance. You compare, analyze and define with logic. But you can only know a thing spiritually by feeling it, becoming it, and allowing your present self to die.

I'm not talking about your physical death. I'm talking about your transformation: changing your concept of yourself with a committed decision. Your transformations begin with an assumption. This new assumption is at a different vibrational frequency than your current state. When you accept a new assumption, you rise to a different state. Just like Harry Potter accepting he had to die to be reborn to kill part of Voldemort. He did not want to die, but he accepted his fate. You want to pay attention to how this assumption process works.

It's completely natural to want more, to expect growth in your sales and business. If you had revenues of a million last year, it is natural to want two million this year. But the man, woman, or business that generates two million a year is not operating under the same ideas and thoughts as those who generate one million a year. Your sales results, goals, and dreams manifest with gestation periods. What manifests depends upon what is in the male and female components of the garden. It's the mixture of these two components that produce our results. This garden grows either by default or by design.

To better understand gestation, let's use the Gardener's mindset. An educated gardener is conscious of four things. Cardinal rule number one, you can never force growth. Force negates. Everything must unfold naturally in its due time, just like a sunflower. Certain knowledge, experience, and building blocks must be acquired along the way.

Second, gardeners check the soil before they plant. They understand there is a time to give and a time to take from the soil. They test for the presence of macro and micronutrients and the neutrality of the soil. The structure of the soil is important to ensure aeration, oxygen flow, and drainage. Evidence of life in the soil is a good indicator of the soil's readiness to plant. Gardeners like to see an abundance of earthworms. That indicates the presence of beneficial microorganisms in the soil.

Third, gardeners prepare the place for the crops to grow. They understand the importance of environment and surroundings. You wouldn't plant sunflower seeds under a dogwood tree and by the azaleas that like acidic soil. Choose environments that provide sources of light, love, care, and warmth; conditions that are in alignment for that plant to grow with ease. Gardeners provide adequate space for the plant to grow to maturity; you don't want to crowd the plants. You consider the size the tree will be at its maturity and make sure there is enough space in the soil for it to establish roots. Gardeners also recognize they will need to add elements of protection and defense to mitigate any weeds or "dis-ease" from disturbing the plants or negatively impacting the harvest.

Finally, after all the preparation, gardeners allow nature to do her part. They have patience and expect a natural unfolding before the harvest. It will come if they put in the proper work up front. They have faith in Nature.

Master gardeners invest time to study. They recognize that they will get better with experience. They apply the knowledge, test it like a scientist, and leverage those experiences to increase their harvest yields.

Unlike everything else in nature that has a pre-designated patterned plan, we can choose what we want to grow into. We can choose the results we would like to manifest. Humans can plant anything they choose in the imagination. Through the use of their imagination, they can transform themselves and their results at any time. Knowing anything is possible is what makes selling so much fun!

True sales professionals are always activating their clients' imaginations, planting visions in the clients' minds, and creating value in harmony with their clients' desires. Your goals, and your clients' goals, are spiritual seeds. The exact gestation period is not always known, but gestation must occur after conception. Spiritual seeds and possibilities are infinite with the imagination. The good thing about operating within the guidelines of nature's law, following the path of "allowance," is that nature loves speed.

So, let's apply these gardeners' rules to selling.

First things first, you must decide what you want to plant, or you'll have a plot of land full of weeds. This decision or lack of decision is the male energy. You can't force growth or force your sales to happen; you must allow them to happen. Be gentle on yourself. Stop beating yourself up. Build yourself up. Repetition is the mother of learning. Practice your sales presentation. Play the "I'm new" card while you can. Be curious about your prospects. Get super interested in them. Begin with the end in mind. Ask yourself, how can I be of service? Who do I want to become in the process of moving toward my end goal? Use an intention to support yourself.

An intention is something that is framed in the positive. It focuses on what you want, makes you responsible for the outcome, and inspires you to act. It's in the present tense, and it's bigger than any one goal. It empowers you. It defines the character traits you want to embody. For example, "My intention is to shower myself in unconditional love throughout this process, to focus on the end, remember why I choose this path, to be present in the moment, and to remind myself to ask which step will take me forward." Allow yourself to bloom and unfold where you are planted.

Two, perform the soil check. Healthy soil means a healthy harvest. A soil test gives you the pH value and the nutrients. Perfect soil is easily workable and porous to allow for aeration. Compact soil is difficult to maintain and does not support life. This is the female energy for conception.

Personally, I like to start with an attitude checkup then proceed with a territory and market soil test. Your attitude is your energy field. It's what you bring to the party! Attitude is the composite of your thoughts, feelings, and actions. Attitude not only affects you but also the people around you, how your clients respond and react toward you. Most people mirror one another. If a customer is nice to you, you are nice to them. But what if they're rude? Are you in the habit of giving them back what they give you? Or have you decided that no matter what anyone on the outside gives you, you are bringing your ten out of ten to the party?

Assess your pH level or attitude on the polarity meter. Are you making positive assumptions or negative assumptions? Your assumptions are the cause of your reality and your results.

If you're making negative assumptions, what would you need to notice, appreciate, or believe to see the good in the situation? The more you look toward the positive, the more positive you will attract. People with positive attitudes draw people toward them. Positive assumptions, connect and join; negative assumptions, constrict and separate.

Aeration: how open minded am I? Ideas and thoughts are the electrons in your garden. If you are not getting the results you want, allow yourself the re-evaluate the ideas and let go of any ideas that don't empower you. Ask yourself, "What ideas am I rejecting that I should be accepting? What ideas am I accepting to be true that I should be rejecting?" If a colleague or manager offers you a new idea on how to get more prospects in your sales funnel, do you evaluate it? Or immediately reject it?

I find these two strategies helpful for opening your mind. One, play the "Yes, and" game. When someone presents an idea, remember that no matter what the idea is, at least 10% of it is right. Focus on the ten percent of the idea that you like. Say, "What I like about that idea is, and I have an idea on how I can use that to build another idea." You do two things here: you get in the practice of looking for what is good or right. And you let the other person feel they were heard. You acknowledge them. You connect.

Instead of asking yourself whether a new idea is right or wrong, ask if the new idea will aide you in pursuing your goal. Does the new idea make you happy? Does it feel good? If the answer is no, graciously release it. If you like, try it on! You are a divine being; your essence is love and happiness. Use your emotions to guide you. Search for a new idea and belief that will empower you. Who is doing what you want to do and making it happen? Who is selling the most? Who is getting the results you want? What ideas are they accepting or rejecting? Be curious, connect, and ask. People are always willing to help you.

Earl Nightingale talked about cutting away all the fetters of the mind and permitting it to soar as it was divinely designed to do. Your emotional mind is your heart center. The more open it is, the more your true essence can expand and flow through it. A good practice of aeration is belief re-evaluations. Fetters are the chains, limitations, and attachments we imposed on ourselves during our domestication process. In the domestication process we created our inner critic to self-domesticate ourselves with judgement. When we judge ourselves or circumstances, that is not our true essence; it is the saboteur we created.

Have empathy with yourself and others. We've all been domesticated with beliefs and ideas we thought were true. But we need to wake up and activate our sage, align ourselves on our happiness channel and put away our Linus safety blankets. We are responsible to clean up our garden, pull out the weeds, the assumptions and beliefs that don't serve us, and only allow those thoughts that make our hearts sing with happiness and joy. If the weeds in your garden are out of control, get some help. Hire a mentor or coach. Some of those weeds are like thistle, they run deep; you need to get at the whole root network to remove it. If your soil is compacted with roots from the weeds, your outdated beliefs, then you won't have enough space for the new beliefs.

Bob Proctor refers to these fetters as paradigms, a multitude of beliefs and habits that regulate your performance and rob you of your dreams. If you feel you have hit a wall or a glass ceiling in your sales results, it's the weeds in the garden of your subconscious mind that need attention. Be kind to yourself. Allow yourself to re-evaluate your beliefs and blow up the ones that don't serve you. If you don't change them, you have gone as far as you will ever go, and you will stay in the prison of your self-imposed limitations.

Now that you've weeded the garden; it's time to plant the new seedlings. This is called preparing the place. Feed the new beliefs and starve the weeds. When the weeds try to make a come-back, say, "Out of here!" Be vigilant and protect your garden. Be patient with yourself and nurture your new beliefs like little seedlings.

The new beliefs require a gestation period too. Give them daily care. You want to simulate your sales presentations daily in your imagination. Prepare your sales presentation. Write it out! Know what weeds or objections you will need to pull out of your client's garden. You can affirm and strengthen your new beliefs with prosperity affirmations. The fastest way to manifest belief is by assumption. Ask yourself, "Now that it is done, I have what I want, how does it feel?"

This is where the rubber meets the road. Conception cannot occur unless the male energy, your goal or desire, is impressed into the dirt of your subconscious mind, the female energy. Everything is dependent upon your concept, your conception of yourself, what you assume and accept to be true. It is the belief that causes the state of expectancy.

Logic is for the mental plane. Do the illogical and act as if your wish is fulfilled. This is how you impress your spiritual seed into the dirt of your subconscious mind. Assume the feeling until it consumes you. Go to your imagination and visualize the end repeatedly. Repetition combined with images from your vision is what causes the new idea to take root. That new feeling is at a vibrational frequency that's different from where you are now. This is pre-cognition, preparing the place.

The psychological forward motion proceeds the physical forward motion. You can experience the feeling now, which is the unconditional part of manifesting before the condition appears. Feeling is what activates the conception and starts the gestation. Ask yourself, "Now that it is done, how do I feel?" Decide to get aligned with your happiness. Surrender to the fact there is a gestation process. The how and timing is not your business. What is your business is to "feel" it is done and act in a state of expectancy. Vibration precedes manifestation. Everything is created twice. This is the power of assumption.

Allow nature to do her part. Your subconscious mind is extremely creative. As soon as you get your garden of thoughts in order with belief and positive assumption, you activate the magnetism in your plot of land; that is called the Law of Attraction. Everything will be revealed, and the seeds you planted will create new results. Act as if it is already done because it is. You have a garden in your mind that is your heart center, through which the essence of your spirit flows, and through which you experience your reality. You can use the garden of your mind to sell more.

Now that you have your sales mindset in order, combine your positive attitude and critical thinking skills to look at your business like it is soil. You want sales of your product and service to grow. So here is what you must do:

1) Decide what harvest you want to reap this year. What is the amount of commission or net profit you want? Be specific like choosing the seeds to plant in a garden. Over plan or "lotsa" commission is not specific. Clarity is essential. Write it down -look at it daily. Affirm it.

2) Give up force and resistance. Accept and allow gestation to occur through your intention.

3) Soil check - Where is the most fertile ground where the action is, where the worms are moving around? Where is the low hanging fruit? What clients are in growth mode or trouble mode? Who is my ideal client? Where do they hang out? What problem do

they have that I solve? What am I really selling? Is my story drawing them in? How does my product or service bring order to where disorder exists and solve the problem they have?

4) Aeration – Master your sales presentation; know the objections, be ready to plant the anti-virus to the objections during your sales presentation to aerate the soil of your clients' mind.

5) Plant the seedlings and prepare the place– get into massive action! Establish a process of urgency and faith. Sow the seeds; accept gestation takes time for seeds to unfold and that you do not sow and reap in the same season. Always be sowing, giving, creating more value. You have existing customers, referrals, new customers, and prospects. Establish a robust cycle and system of prospecting, presenting, and follow up for closure.

Love your dirt! Your mind, your dirt, is your greatest asset – use it! Embrace and enjoy the process of the gestation period. You can create anything in your dirt. Become the Master Gardner of your mind!

Chapter XI – Calibrate Yourself to the Frequency of Bliss and Ease!

The Law of Least Effort and the Law of Detachment

"An integral being knows without going, sees without looking, and accomplishes without doing." – Lao Tzu

- "If you are one of those who believe that hard work and honesty, alone, will bring riches, perish the thought! It is not true! Riches, when they come in huge quantities, are never the result of HARD work! Riches come, if they come at all, in response to definite demands, based upon the application of definite principles, and not by chance or luck. - Napoleon Hill

- Yesterday is history. Tomorrow is a mystery, but today is a gift! That is why it is called the present. ' Master Oogway

What if it can be easy? Well, it can be, it is only a matter of choice. If you think it's hard you are right; if you think it is easy, it is! Your life is your virtual reality. Think of yourself as a projector and your beliefs, assumptions and perceptions are films, something you can pull from the shelf as the director and put into the projector. Whatever movie you want to play will show up on the screen. If that analogy doesn't work for you, try this one on. Imagine you have a shelf full of glasses with different colored lenses. You can pull any pair off the shelf and put them on – put on the rose-colored ones and see rose colored pictures. Put on the green ones and see green colored pictures. What Wayne Dyer said is true. "When we change, they we look at things, the things we look at change." Easy or hard is nothing more than a choice.

But you say no, life is hard. I want to let you in on a secret. Somewhere between the time of Adam and Eve up until today, an idea got planted and accepted in man's mind that life is hard. That life is happening to us instead of for us. And it has been passed on for years. Any idea accepted becomes a belief. It does not mean it is fact and truth.

I want to challenge the idea that work and selling are hard. If you bought into that idea and believe the "hard" part, I want you to recognize there is a virus code in your programming. Now if the idea of "hard" work empowers you and juices you up, by all means hold onto it; you may want to come back to this chapter in another five or ten years.

But if you have been at this work and selling thing for twenty or thirty years and have become exhausted from being on the hamster wheel going through the motions, bumping up against walls and glass ceilings, and not getting the results you deeply desire, I suggest you stay with me here and take a second look at the idea of "work" and the adjective you want to put before the word to describe it.

As children we operated in bliss and ease. We were not wringing our hands, worrying about what anyone thought of us, who we had to please, how to avoid conflict, or how we were going to accomplish something. Nope, we were just "being" right in the present moment, absorbing it all in and enjoying the splendor of the experience. We are born risk-takers, fearless, fueled with curiosity, enthusiasm, and love. We lived in a state of bliss and ease up until ......the time that the adults around us started saying, *"How can you be that happy? Who do you think you are? Life doesn't work like that. You must work hard if you want to succeed. You want a new bike or video game or new outfit and shoes. How do you plan to get it? You can't always get what you want. That's just the way life is."* Sound familiar?

Nonresistant thought is bliss. True bliss is in complete harmony with who you are. But what causes you to resist bliss? You convinced yourself you are unworthy of it. Why? Because you think you need to calibrate to the others outside of you who suffer. The irony is humans calibrate themselves to their problems instead of their bliss.

When we got socialized and domesticated, we were told, "That's not the way life goes. Life is hard. Toughen up!" Consider accepting a new idea. The value you can be to others is contrast – evolution of the species. It's easy to calibrate to what is on the outside. It takes mastery to calibrate to your dreams and be in complete alignment with who you are. Mastery takes an unwillingness to feel bad. It is as simple as this: feel good. When you are giving you feel good! Try that on.

When we were children, we never worried about the "how." As little kids, we had persistence. We just kept asking for what we wanted. It was not until school started, that by rapid fire, the adults started asking us for explanations on "how?" That is when we started to question ourselves. As children we were confident and expected whatever was needed would show up when we needed it. Remember?

Domestication taught us conditional love. We longed for approval and wanted to fit in with the crowd. Not knowing any better, we fell in line and accepted the ideas we heard. We traded bliss and ease for approval. It was deductive reasoning, Monkey See, Monkey Do. The unfortunate consequence of this virus code is it is still affecting most of us today. We have not examined our programing. No one taught us that we have mental faculties that can alter the programs of habit in our emotional mind. As a result, when we do not know "how" to get something we want, we let our dreams die and settle for what we have. The "Life and work is hard" line was repeated and suggested so often that it has become a habitual form of thought and we believe it. But is it really true?

Success does require work and action but more importantly it requires critical thinking. Let's open up our critical thinking tool box of: **analysis, interpretation, inference, explanation, self-regulation, open-mindedness, and problem-solving**, and use these skills to re-examine the difference between hard work and easy work to see what is the best fit for today.

Analysis of Work. The noun states, *"activity involving mental or physical effort done in order to achieve a purpose or result; a task or tasks to be undertaken; something a person or thing has to do."* The verb states, *"be engaged in physical or mental activity in order to achieve a result; operate or function, especially properly or effectively."* In physics work is *"energy transferred to or from an object via the application of force along a displacement."*

Only you can express your unique gift in your unique way. You have important work to do, your definite purpose, your dharma. Try on this idea. You were not made for work; work was made for you to express your unique talents, your purpose. Work is a place for you to be engaged, be effective, and create results. When you are authentic, present, and free to be yourself, you can just "be" without effort. When you do what you love to do, something you are in resonance with, judgement lessens, engagement increases and fulfillment, adventure, joy, and bliss show up. You are back on your happiness frequency. You feel connection and your creativity is activated. Your life and work become effortless, just like what you observe in nature.

Nature's intelligence functions with effortless ease; it is carefree; it operates with an intention of harmony and in a spirit of love. Observe nature and you will see no effort is being expended. Grass is not struggling to grow, it just grows. Birds do not struggle to fly, they just fly. Cut yourself some roses, put them in a vase of water; and watch them bloom, they don't struggle to open up. You don't have to force yourself to breathe, you just breathe. You are a powerful force of nature. It is your divine right, to be fully self-expressed as the true authentic you, and manifest your dreams in physical form with ease in an effortless way. All you have to do is claim it.

But why do we believe it is hard? Because you have accepted a lie to be true for you. The virus program inside your mind is the only thing that is holding you back. The virus program or belief warns you the path to success is "hard." The warning causes your attention to look for the struggle instead of the bliss and you find whatever you look for. Where your attention flows the energy goes.

Price Pritchard in the book, "*You2*" uses the analogy of a fly burning out its energy in a futile attempt to fly through the glass of a window pane. All that energy and hard work causes the fly to be doomed. Yet 10 feet away, and 10 seconds of flying time would allow the fly to easily go out the door. The point is don't try harder, try another approach. If you think selling is hard, you are right; if you think selling is easy, it is!

Let's look at the adjectives. HARD in the dictionary means *"solid and strong; done with a great deal of force or strength."* EASY means *"achieved without great effort; presenting few difficulties; free from worries or problems."* Hard is on one side of the polarity pole; Easy is on the other. You get to choose where to focus your attention. It's the contrast that allows you to decide and the beauty is you can always make a different choice.

Force and resistance negate; think of resistance as a negative sign in a math problem; Use the grade school explanation, a negative is *"taking something away from"*; That something is your energy. As you choose and evaluate, ask yourself, "Am I more empowered by a belief in going three steps backwards before one step forward? Or would it be easier just to go forward?"

Humans have the power to consciously decide what interpretation or meaning they will place on anything. That interpretation, perception, or meaning creates a vibration or feeling. The truth about life is, life just is. We make it what we want it to be. Humans are meaning making machines and can focus their attention at will. Interpretations are analogous to a film or a set of glasses that regulate how you see your world.

If you accept the idea that work and selling is hard, you will view your world through the lens of difficulty, looking for why it will be hard; you will direct your attention to find struggle. Don't you think starting off with the perception that selling is going to be hard is affecting your intention and outcome? Perhaps making you nervous? Causing anxiety? Now think. Why would it be hard to go to a sales call, meet another human being with curiosity looking for an opportunity to serve and engage in that conversation? What would you need to notice, or appreciate to believe to feel it is easy? Where would you need to direct your attention if I told you, it was easy?

We are all living in our own virtual reality. We either live from the inside out or the outside in. It took me a while to really understand what that means. This is the best way I have found to explain it to my clients, family, and loved ones. We have a spiritual side and a physical side. An invisible side and a visible side to ourselves. It's almost like looking at a half dollar. You can only focus and see one side of the coin at a time. The heads side of the coin states "In God we trust" and has the word Liberty on it. Let's call that your spiritual side. The tails side has the symbol for the USA, the eagle. Let's call that your physical side, it's the symbol of you. The question becomes what side of the coin will you lean into for your point of support? Will your balance, your decisions, and your consciousness depend on something internal, like your spiritual side or something external, like the symbol side?

All of our experiences and sales scenarios have two factors – ourselves and the matter to be dealt with. If you feel weight on you from the matter to be dealt with, the sale to be made, that weight and heaviness you feel is a signal, feedback made for you, that you are leaning into the outside for support; that's why it's hard. You've given your power away to the external situation or circumstance. You've become detached from your internal power source. You are living from the outside in.

If you have a light, playful handling of the circumstance you have a firm grasp and perfect control over it. You are touching lightly, like a butterfly sitting on a flower, able to move and fly about freely. You are leaning into your inner power for support. You have power in reserve, and an abundance of it. That is why it is easy. You are in the flow. You have not wasted any energy; you are light, not taking anything too seriously, just enjoying the experience and being in a field of possibility to create.

There are two Spiritual Laws of Success that can explain how to maintain your internal point of support and tune yourself back into the frequency of bliss and ease with which you entered this world.

The Law of Least Effort, one of seven spiritual laws of success, is the principle of taking least action, which means – take the path of no resistance. The path of acceptance is no resistance and means "do less, be more and accomplish more.

Face it, whatever you resist, persists. Resistance requires energy. The belief of Least Effort is that the lack of resistance is what causes your success. You are able to hold more energy in reserve. The Law of Least Effort reveals that regardless of what situation or circumstance comes your way, there is always an opportunity for you to create in this new field of possibility. Least effort is hurry without haste. Know everything you encounter along your journey of life contains a gift. There are no failures or losses, or mistakes, just lessons. Lessons are for your evolution. If you resist a lesson, the lesson will keep showing up until you accept the lesson as a gift. Acceptance is the gateway for your freedom.

In Neville Goddard's book, *"The Power of Awareness,"* Neville defines the physics principle of Least action as the minimum energy multiplied by the minimum of time. Neville states we can employ the psychological equivalent of Least Action by assumption. Assumption happens in your imagination. Assumption is as simple as dreaming that you are already where you want to be and asking yourself, now that I am here how do I feel? Easy.

Remember all your assumptions are causing your life. You put the film in your movie projector or the glasses on your face. You have the power to choose. When you focus your attention on where you want to be without effort that means you relax and LET or allow it to happen. Attention minus effort equals "LET." Allow the experience to unfold. We touched on this with the Law of Gestation.

Einstein's formula referenced "ease" as traveling with the speed of light. You can travel at the speed of light in your imagination – it can take you anywhere. James Allen wrote words of wisdom in his book *"As a Man Thinketh."* He stated, *"As you think you travel, and as you love you attract. You are today where your thoughts brought you; you will be tomorrow where your thoughts take you."*

I believe our thoughts enable us to travel by the speed of light. If I ask you about the pots and pans in your kitchen, what they look like in detail, you travel to your kitchen. If I ask you about your dream vacation in Europe you go right to that moment when you are in Rome eating all that delicious food and wine. If your dream vacation was with the grandkids in Disney or Universal studios, you can immediately transport yourself to Florida or California. You are always going on thought trips. Thought trips are easy, not hard. Attraction is easy as well. Love is resonance and causes attraction. Trust what you are attracting.

But you say I'm not attracting what I want, perhaps you really are. Life is happening for you. You want to be in the flow but you are not. That contrast is a message. Listen to it. What would you love? You are always making choices based on what you love or what you believe you need to choose to preserve love. The results are feedback. Feedback comes by the emotions you feel. Intuition is feedback in the absence of fear. It is the contrast of polarity that helps us choose wisely. If the first choice doesn't work out, you can learn from it and make another choice.

Are you involved in something you love to do, selling something you love? Or have you chosen duty over love? Listen to your heart, do not ignore it. You can always make another choice and change direction. You have the power.

You ask, but how do I "do less and accomplish more?"

The Law suggests that there are three components to "Least Effort." The first component requires a commitment to Acceptance. This means you are committed to accept every moment is as it should be because the whole universe is as it should be. You are not the ocean, you are a wave, a center for distribution connected to something bigger than yourself.

Now if you are feeling uncomfortable with the commitment to accepting things as they are, ask yourself what about that statement is making you uncomfortable? Perhaps you just lost a sale, or you got a quota that you believe is unattainable, or you have no new products to sell, or you have been told you have to attend a sales meeting and lose a weekend at home with your family? Or your sales dried up and you can't meet the payroll or pay your bills. And you say, "Why in the world would I want to accept that?

Pay close attention. I am not asking you to settle for what is, and not wish for a different future. I know you are the change agent! I am just asking you to accept things as they are *in this moment* and to *take your power back in the moment*. Sometimes the contrast in life is the only way we learn or wake up. When you struggle against the moment, you are actually struggling against the whole universe and that's why it is hard. Realize what you are actually reacting to. You are not reacting to the circumstance or a person's actions out there; You are reacting to your feelings about the person or the situation. Your emotions are your vibrational translator. Resisting that emotion is negation, putting you in reverse, taking your energy away. Your feelings belong to you and are not someone else's fault. Instead of resisting what is, ask yourself, "What can I do in this moment to make me feel good? Do I want to direct my attention, to what is, what I see on the physical plane which is a result of my past thinking? Or do I want to direct my attention towards what I want and create something new?" If you can accept things as they are in the moment, you are ready to assume your "response" ability. You are ready to respond versus react.

The second component for "do less and accomplish more" is responsibility. This means taking your power back, having the ability to have a creative response to the situation as it is now in the present. This is looking for the gift, the seed of opportunity in the field of possibility. Taking your power back is having confidence in your ability to make lemonade from the lemons; It is your ability to transform whatever is in front of you with ease. Remember, your reality is nothing more than an interpretation. Life is happening *FOR* you. The Law states that we need to be reminded that, "This moment is exactly as it should be. It is precisely the one you need to serve your own evolution." It's the storms that often break us open and wash us clean. It is the storms that allow that big dog within to come out.

The third component of Least Effort is defenselessness, be comfortable in your beliefs; meaning relinquishing the need to convince or persuade anyone towards your point of view. This is not a sign of weakness but a sign of strength. Doing this gives you access to enormous amounts of energy that was previously wasted. What is gained by being defensive, blaming, and refusal to accept the present moment as it is? Your resistance and force will produce an outcome similar to the rigidity of a tall oak that collapses in the storm.

Look at what happened during the pandemic. The people and businesses' who remained flexible like a reed that can bend in the storm survived and thrived. It makes sense if you think about it; when you have no point to defend, you have no argument. You have harmony. You experience the present as a gift. Harmony is trading appreciation for expectation. You begin to see the spirit in everything that is alive. You feel the spirit of life in you and become carefree, experience joy and freedom. You discover what you want is available at any time, you can give it to yourself. Aligning with your happiness channel becomes habitual. The path of zero resistance is the path to easy.

The second law that allows you to calibrate yourself to the frequency of bliss and ease is the Law of Detachment.

Detachment contains the wisdom of uncertainty and freedom from the past. Detachment is the key that unlocks you from the prison of limitations from your past conditioning. Surrender is the willingness to let go and step into the unknown, a new field of possibility; to surrender our individual control to the creative mind, infinite intelligence, that orchestrates the dance of the universe and trust. It is being humble. Remembering your place in the universe. You are not the source energy that does the work. You are a center of distribution that channels the power.

Here is what the law of detachment means. Receiving on the physical plane occurs by relinquishment of any attachment to the physical symbol you want to create. This does not mean you give up any intention to create your desire, you just give up attachment to the result the way you expect it to be. You definitely expect it but are not attached to the HOW. The how is not your business. Sometimes the universe has a better plan than what you come up with on your own. Detachment is based on an unquestioning belief in the power of your true Self. Know whatever you ask for is coming to you. If you want it faster get out of your own way. Become receptive.

Here's the problem with attachment. Attachments are like fly paper. They restrict your movement. Attachments are based on insecurity and fear. Attachment is the feeling that you might lose something and won't be able to get it back. Security is an ephemeral thing. Looking for security outside of you is an illusion. As a child it may have been okay to suck our thumbs and carry around a security blanket like Linus from the Peanuts gang; but if we are going to act like adults and grow up, we need to let go.

I can't tell you how many times I meet with people in corporate America that choose to stay in a job they hate for security. They will say, "I will pursue my dream after I have X Million dollars in the bank. Then I will be financially independent and retire or start my new business." But the sad thing is it never happens. They chase security for a lifetime and never find it. And they die with their dreams left inside them;

the dreams they never get to experience because they bought into an illusion of security and safety.

When you are attached, your intention and mindset is locked and narrow in what is or already has been. You lose fluidity, creativity, and spontaneity. Attachment interferes with the whole process of creation. Security and certainty are attachments to the known. That means no new creation! If you have no evolution, you experience stagnation, complacency, entropy, disorder and decay. Wouldn't you rather have adventure, excitement, and fulfillment?

The answer to your freedom is in the wisdom of insecurity and uncertainty. Uncertainty is where your freedom to create exists; it is the pathway towards your evolution. In uncertainty you are less likely to "force" solutions on problems. Forcing solutions on problems only creates more problems. Lack of force means you will not be wasting energy in negation. You have more energy to create your bliss with ease.

The Law of Detachment states that all wealth, abundance or anything in the physical world comes from your inner power, your spirit being fused with universal intelligence. Everything on the physical plane is a symbol. And symbols come and go; they are transitory just like the roles we assume in life at different times. Those who have the most wisdom realize that if they created something once, they can create it again and make it even better. People who adopt a prosperity consciousness realize this fact and understand they have infinite freedom to create.

I'm sure you have witnessed people or businesses in the news who experienced a big loss and then came back from it. Take a corporation like Johnson and Johnson. The Tylenol scandal may have set them back temporarily but they rebounded right back using their creativity. They understood from remembering their past success, that they have the ability to create anything they want, anytime they want, and with the least effort. Or watch the Rocky movies, those are classic stories of comebacks, stories we all love because it gives us hope. It feels good to watch and experience that feeling.

In contrast, those who come from a poverty consciousness are always chasing symbols, holding on to the past, missing out on the opportunities in the present, going in the opposite direction of progress. Complacency causes replacement. Law states you either create or disintegrate. And scarcity doesn't feel good. Listen to your heart's clues – if it doesn't feel good, you are going in the wrong direction.

What others call good luck is nothing more than a result of being prepared, living from the field of uncertainty, embracing the infinite game, looking for the good, and knowing that seeds of opportunity are everywhere. It is the habit of asking what is the gift here? What is good? How can I use my talents to create a solution of evolutionary benefit for all concerned?

When we operate in alignment with nature's principle and law, by least effort, without attachment, in the spirit of harmony and love, life is easy, and so is selling. Harmony is without resistance and love is resonance.

At this point we have re-evaluated the difference between hard and easy. Now it's time for you to choose how do you want to view selling, through the lens of hard or easy? If you are making a transition from hard to easy the best way to tune into your bliss and ease frequency is the daily practice Gratitude! Appreciating all that is good, all of your blessings.

Neville Goddard described gratitude as the coin of heaven. You can experience your heaven on earth through gratitude. Neville said the coin of heaven is an immortal gift, having two sides, Mind and speech. Controlling our inner dialogue is key. We have inner conversations daily. Make "thank you" your catch phrase. When you radiate and live gratitude, the Universe will respond in abundance. The universe will match the intensity of your gratitude. Easy will get even easier. Gratitude expands relationships, improves physical and psychological health; it enhances empathy, sleep; it reduces aggression, improves self-esteem, and increases mental strength.

So, there you have it. Live by the Laws of Least Effort and Detachment and choose easy. You are a spiritual being and you have an internal guidance system. Listen to your heart. Choose the feel-good experiences, create them and you will have regained your power to stay on the frequency of bliss and ease.

Less is more.

Chapter XII – Take Your Power Back and Find Your Way Home

The Law of Use

"The Greatest Sin of Mankind: Neglect to use his greatest asset." – Napoleon Hill

Have you ever been sucked into a high drama situation during your sales career? It may have happened inside the company, with a client, or amongst your colleagues. Your company gets a new CEO; the company is sold; the company gets bought; the company goes out of business. You interview for an internal promotion and you get it or perhaps you don't; You get a new manager; There is a hiring freeze; there is massive hiring effort; Someone you know gets fired or laid off; Someone leaves unexpectantly; There is a large-scale reduction in force; Your company undergoes a re-organization. A pandemic explodes. On and on it goes right?

It's amazing how some of these circumstances can cause our attention and focus to drift off of our path and onto a stage in someone else's movie with high drama, excitement, and fear in a few seconds. Everything can be going smooth as silk and all of a sudden BOOM! Everything you were just enjoying is all turned upside down. And then we find our focus being pulled in a Tug of War of contradictions which means you've got momentum going in two different directions and as a result you get stuck. How does this happen and what is really going on?

Momentum is where the action is. You are a vibrational being who is drawn toward action. Remember the coin analogy I gave you earlier? You have two sides to yourself just like a coin. One side of the coin says "In God We Trust," think of that as your spiritual side; the other side has the symbol, the eagle on it, your physical side. You vibrate and move on both sides of your "being" highways. You can experience momentum on your spiritual side by using your mental faculties to create and you can experience momentum on the physical side by getting drawn into the ISNESS you observe. You can spiral up or down in the momentum. The only way to maintain balance is to stay close to your center of gravity.

Picture yourself traveling on your journey crossing back and forth between two highways, chasing the momentum. When you cross from one lane to the other if you pay attention, you can "feel" the rumble strip and "feel" the emotions you have on either lane of momentum. You can feel the loss of your center of gravity when you wander too far away from your internal source of power. That's when things feel like they are spiraling out of control and you feel the weight of the outside on you. You can also feel the "flow" when everything is moving in a positive state. You are tuned in and tapped into your courage, confidence, competence; you are light, and maintaining your center of gravity.

The question is are you consciously choosing which lane you are in and how long you intend to stay in that lane based on how you feel? Here's the deal - the lane you give the most focus to will gain the most momentum and pull you. Where your attention goes, the energy flows.

The two lanes represent two points of attraction for you; that of your inner being and that of your physical being. You are always attracting with your attention. In one lane you wield all the power, in the other lane you give it away.

Why do you think most people are not deliberate about where they place their focus? You could say most people are "reacting" instead of "responding." Really not thinking because they are not consciously choosing their thoughts. But do you know why? We are vibrational beings and our tendency and habits are to drawn toward the satisfaction of momentum. That's why people suffer from fear of missing out or the shiny object syndrome. They have no controlled attention, but rather love excitement and action. It's easier to focus on existing momentum than it is to create your own new momentum; at least until you become aware of what's going on. Controlled attention requires self-discipline.

Let me provide you an example we can all relate to. Sit in your observer seat with me and let's revisit the movie, "*The Wizard of Oz.*" Dorothy is an orphaned teenager living on a farm in Kansas. On the way home from school her dog Toto chases after Miss Gulch's cat. Miss Gulch hits her dog Toto on the back with a rake which causes Toto to bite Miss Gulch. Miss Gulch is a prominent land owner who owns half the property in the town. Dorothy runs home to tell her aunt, uncle, and the farm aides what happened to Toto but no one has time to listen to her story. They have work to get done on the farm. They tell Dorothy to stay out of trouble. Dorothy then starts dreaming of going "somewhere over the rainbow" to a place where all her dreams can come true.

Meanwhile, Miss Gulch was so irritated that she obtained a permit from the sheriff's office to retrieve the dog. Miss Gulch shows up at Aunt Em and Uncle Henry's front door with a permit to remove the dog. She threatens that if Aunt Em and Uncle Henry do not comply with the permit, she will come after their farm. Dorothy's Aunt and Uncle do not want to break the law or risk losing their farm so they surrender the dog to Miss Gulch who storms out of the house with the dog, puts it in her bike basket, and pedals down the road. Toto the dog jumps out of the basket and runs back to Dorothy who is in her room crying.

Dorothy is elated to have Toto back but her thought immediately shifts to the fear of losing Toto again. She decides to run away with Toto. Dorothy meets up with a phony fortune teller on the road who realizes Dorothy is trying to run away. He looks in his crystal ball and tells Dorothy that her Aunt Em is crying and her heart is broken. Dorothy is moved by compassion for her aunt and rushes to return home. On her way home a tornado storm hits! As Dorothy attempts to find her aunt in the storm cellar, she gets hit on the head with a window and falls unconscious in the house. In her dream, she gets whisked away to the Land of Oz. All through the dream she tries to find her way home seeking the answer "out there" from a wizard, only to find out at the end of the movie that she has always had the power to get herself home without any assistance. She learns at the end of the movie that her heart's desire is at home.

I want to talk to you about how you can find your way home to where your inner power resides, where all your desires, happiness and freedom exists. I want to show you why and when you give your power away so you can *consciously* be aware of the traps and choose to maintain your power in all circumstances. The journey towards your greater awareness and mastery of self requires discovering your courage, following your heart, and taking full control of your greatest asset, your marvelous mind. This is about empowerment; No surrender.

To illustrate my point about your tendency to follow momentum, pay attention to how Dorothy's focus is predominantly on herself and how her attention moves back and forth from what she wants to what she doesn't want.

- *First scene:* Toto chases cat, gets hit on the back with a rake and then bites the neighbor. **Thought** – outrage, injustice, someone hear me. (**Feeling** - anger) **Action** – Seek help.

- *Second scene:* Adults busy on farm; Dorothy told to go where she will not get into trouble. **Thought-**Somewhere over the rainbow– adventure (**Feeling** - Happy! Hope & belief) **Action** – Dream.

- *Scene 3*: Gulch, Dorothy's villain shows up and takes the dog. **Thought** – She's a wicked witch! (**Feeling**s - Fear and sadness from loss/love for her dog); Action - cry

- *Scene 4* – Toto returns! – **Thought** – Relief! (**Feeling** Hope & joy) **Action**: Hug

  Followed by **Next thought** – Gulch will come back! – (**Feeling** - fear) – **Action** -run away!

- *Scene 5* – Meets Fortune Teller – **Thought** – Go on adventure! (**Feeling** - Hope & belief); **Action**: consult crystal ball

- *Scene 6*– Crystal Ball reading -Aunt Em heart broken – **Thought** – I didn't want to hurt her (**Feeling** – Concern/Compassion/ love) – **Action** - Hurry home.

- *Scene 7* – Tornado, **Thought**- Danger; I can't find my loved ones; I'm all alone **(feeling** - fear) **action**: get back in house for safety- BANG on head

- *Scene 8* – Arrival in Oz. **Thought**: I'm not in Kansas anymore; this must be the place over the rainbow. **Feeling**: Uncertainty and excitement **Action:** Follow the yellow brick road.

As you can see before we even get into what happens in Oz, Dorothy's attention was being drawn towards the momentum – where the action was. That is the trap you fall into. Why? You are a vibrational being with a vibrational stance. You are picking up vibrations from your physical senses all the time. You cannot control the seventy thousand thoughts that will bombard you every day but you can control your attention.

As human beings, our tendency and habitual behavior is being drawn into the momentum of our problems. Our dharma, the reason we chose to come into this space-time continuum was to serve. The benefit that comes from being drawn to the problems we experience is we are able to observe and create from the contrast for our evolution. There will always be contrast so you can create. The drawback and mistake most of us make in the process is calibrating ourselves to the problem instead of calibrating ourselves to the solution, our inner being, source energy. In other words what are you getting yourself in alignment with? The inside or the outside? Problems have momentum and resistance. Solutions have momentum with no resistance. See the difference?

Most of us spend too much time in the resistance being calibrated to the subjects that have us paralyzed instead of holding our focus long enough on the solution to allow the solution to start amassing direction and momentum toward what we do want. We seem to have forgotten we came into this world with a GPS that has a thinker to set direction and an emotional guidance system, to help us navigate the path of least resistance! We forget to use our greatest asset to keep us calibrated to our power source. It's our contradictory thoughts that stop momentum and keep us wrapped around the axle. Hesitation kills momentum. If desire is pulling you to the right with positive thought and your belief contradicts your desire and pulls you left with negative thought, disbelief, you are stuck in a state of inertia. You lose momentum. When decisions are made with a closed mind and refusal to learn the truth you remain stuck in ignorance.

The Law of Use states, whatever you don't use, you lose. If you quit, you lose automatically. Ambition unused declines. Faith unused decreases. Vitality or energy unused decreases. You can't save your energy; you must release it. You can't save today and use it at the end of the year. Whatever you do not employ, you forfeit. Your mind works the same way. When you don't use your power, you lose it. It's time to wake up and start putting that power to use!

You ask, "What do you mean when you say I am giving my power away, that I am not plugged into source?" Simply put, you are giving your focus and attention to the momentum "out there" and you let what you observe on the physical plane, the ISNESS, control you. That is how you give your power away. You become like the scarecrow and have forgotten you have a brain controlling your nervous system and the wizard behind that brain is your mind. You've forgotten you have a will and with self-command you can control where you place your focus.

You know when you are "in the zone" selling. Everything is unfolding perfectly. You expect to win! You are operating from your inner power, source energy. You can feel the experience of fulfillment and happiness, you feel good! You have balance and your center of gravity is solid. When you do not feel good, you've crossed over the rumble strip from the inside to the outside, the further away you go from your center of gravity, you lose connection to your power source and become unstable. You are at the effect of something outside of you.

You want to be at the cause of your life and your sales focusing from the invisible vibrational and emotional reality to create. Here is truth. Everything is created twice. We become what we think about. What's on the inside is always being reflected back to you on the outside. Your current sales results are a reflection of what's been going on inside your mind, where you have been placing your attention. Those with awareness on how to use and direct their power are at the cause of their life the majority of the time because they consciously choose where they will channel their power.

What's the secret? How do you build the muscle mastery skills to control your attention and hold onto your power? Use your mental faculties, your invisible powers. Practice. Stop calibrating yourself to others responses to you; instead calibrate yourself to source; your inner power which means think a thought that has no resistance. Start with "I can." Apply Universal Laws to your behavior. Turn on your GPS and start to use it. Viscerally become aware of how to balance desire with belief to put yourself in a state of expectancy. Your desires are always growing and that means your beliefs need to grow as well. Two positives balanced and congruent cause momentum forward. A positive and negative thought mix is contradictory and will hold you in a state of inertia.

Start appreciating the thing in life you received for free – your mind and put it to use! If you think a thought that feels good, you are calibrating to source; if you think a thought that makes you feel bad, you are calibrating to something outside of you. Catch and detect your "off" feeling and "not so good" vibrations early.

Vibration is everything. You are a spiritual being, with an intellect, having a physical experience. You translate vibrations with your emotions. You cause your own virtual reality. Polarity is a tool to help you understand how calibrated to source you are. Nature and life always move in the positive direction. You have a mind. It has two functions; the male energy of the mind sets direction; the female energy of the mind is your emotional translator and your cybernetic guidance system; listen to your heart. Keep moving towards what feels positive.

Take the power quiz. How often are you off to see the wizard? Do you search for answers out there, asking everyone for their opinions? Or do you routinely ask yourself the questions and be silent to hear the answers from your intuition?

Do you readily accept whatever someone tells you? Whatever you hear on TV or by the water cooler? Or do you look for fact and consult the experts instead of gathering opinions?

Are you procrastinating and suffering from indecision? Do you reach decisions slowly and change them quickly and often? Or do you reach decisions quickly and rarely if ever change them? Do you make decisions based on what you have, the "ISNTESS" you see? Or do you make decisions based on what you love because you know the truth that "ISNESS" is created first in your imagination?

Have you lost your voice? Or are you fully self-expressed? Are you still playing Monkey See, Monkey Do? Or do you originate your own direction based on what you want vs what you have?

Have you been burned so many times that you are unwilling to entertain any new ideas? Have you closed your heart for fear of having it broken? Are you holding onto your pain or letting it go? Or are you open to new ideas and willing to re-evaluate yours? Are you willing to feel the contrast and release it so you can appreciate what you have and create something new? Do you suppress your emotions or do you listen to them and express them?

The only reason you ever experience resistance is because you feel threatened. You think you cannot have what you want. It's your disbelief that holds you back. Universal power, your source of supply does not exist in unbelief.

When you begin to calibrate yourself to your joy you will not feel threatened. In that joyful state you allow everyone around you to live and let live. Others are free to create and so are you. The easiest way to create momentum for what you want is to think non-resistant thoughts. It requires an act of applied faith. Use the mental faculty of your will and take action on what you can do now.

You can declare today to become master of your fate and never relinquish your power again. When you align your thoughts with universal laws, thinking on purpose in a state of positive motion forward, you will experience straight up source; your holding tank where all your dreams and hopes are held. You will feel elation, ecstasy. When you are in the state of no resistance you are at the center of your power source. You are home.

But how do I get home you ask. When you feel resistance, you've crossed the rumble strip and are on the outside. Start with a thought that doesn't have resistance to get you headed back home. You must build mental muscle to hold yourself in a vibrational stance of belief and expectation instead of resistance. Trust the power and go to it for everything.

Let's be specific. Let's continue down the yellow brick road with Dorothy and see what lessons she learned. You need to have courage, heart, and brains to sell well. And above all belief.

"If I only had a brain."

At times we can all resonate with the scarecrow. Truth is we are wicked smart but often we forget to use our brain, our critical thinking skills, at least until we are faced with some challenge that demands our remembrance on the spot to put the thinker into action or until someone or something inspires us into action. Before Scarecrow met Dorothy, he was settling, hanging on a post trying to scare the crows away. He knew how to get down from the pole but he was not motivated to do so until Dorothy showed up and shared an idea that inspired him.

When Dorothy first meets the scarecrow, Scarecrow tells her he can't make up his mind. Have you ever said that? "I can't make up my mind." Dorothy asks, "How can you talk without a brain? Scarecrow replies, "Many people do a lot of talking without thinking." Boy, there's wisdom and sarcasm in that statement!

It's the scarecrow who leads the charge to rescue Dorothy from the flying monkeys and devises the plan to get into the castle to rescue her. Scarecrow also shows Dorothy how to get the apples from the trees so she can eat one by telling the trees "Who would want those apples anyway?" The trees then start to hurl their apples at them. Pretty smart hey?

Sometimes we act like the scarecrow when we start to compare ourselves with others and think because we do not have that extra degree, we are not enough. Have you ever felt you were not enough, that something was missing in you? We walk around in an illusion focused on what we think we are *NOT* as opposed to seeing who we really are; the divinity within. Like the Scarecrow we long for some acknowledgement from the outside. In his case, it took the wizard to provide him a diploma, before he claimed his brilliance. Yet he had his brilliance the whole time.

Recognize just how magnificent you are. Focus on what you do well, your strengths. Believe in yourself. Your greatest asset is your mind and you have the power to decide your direction and place your attention and focus towards what will make you happy. You have the ability to calibrate yourself to source energy by thinking non-resistant thoughts. Mornings are a great time to calibrate because your conscious mind took a break while you slept. If you get off track mid-day, take five minutes to meditate or take a walk-in nature and notice the beauty. Relax. Focus on creating instead of comparing yourself to anyone else. You are the only YOU in the universe. You are unique. You have the ability to accept, reject or originate ideas. Use your thinker! The ideas you come up with on your own are your immaculate conceptions. If someone doesn't like them, say, "That's interesting, I see you see it that way." Remember it's your dream, not theirs.

There is no inspiration in settling. There is no inspiration in setting a goal you know how to do or a goal you think you can do. Think BIG. Inspiration causes momentum. Set a goal in a direction that lights up your passion. Feeling good causes momentum. Be at the cause of your life. When you set a goal to grow, to be more, you will want to share what you learn with others. You will think on purpose from a state of non-resistance. You will sell from a state of non-resistance. When you are calibrated to source, your inner power, and find the vibrational stance and attitude of non-resistance you will serve others powerfully and create abundance and prosperity everywhere you go.

"If I were King of the Forest" - Claim Your Courage and wear the badge of honor

Maybe you can relate to the Cowardly Lion. You want to be King of your forest but you lost your voice or haven't found it. Has fear has robbed you of your courage and confidence? Are you at a loss as to how to get it back? Do you feel you are under attack? If so, it's likely you have resorted to your childhood protection strategies.

Perhaps it was one of those changing events I mentioned in the first paragraph that caught you off guard and triggered your loss of confidence? Listen to your inner talk. Did you say to yourself, "I am powerless?" Or "I am not enough?" Ask yourself, "What did my inner critic voice or judge tell me when that happened?" Did that recent situation remind you of something that happened in the past?

If you are suffering like the lion Dorothy met on the yellow brick road you have an inner child within you that needs your attention. You've given your power away to your Judge, your inner child. Everyone has a Judge. The Judge is that voice you hear that you think is you but it's really not you. That voice that tells you, "You are not enough." When the judge in us gets activated, we judge ourselves, others, and circumstances. The judge is the one that robs us of our courage and confidence. We invented this imaginary voice for self-domestication at a young age, when we first learned to rationalize, back somewhere between five and ten years of age. We invented the judge to control our behavior, to keep us safe from things going on around us that we did not fully understand. The Judge and Inner Critic are rooted in fear. They had a purpose and function when we were children, but now as an adult, you cannot afford to give this Judge your power. If you continue to do so, the judge will rob you of your freedom, your spirit. You need a new habit to let your judge know YOU are now in charge.

Symptoms of surrendering you power to the judge include hiding in the shadows, staying out of the limelight, and procrastination. You act like the lion who hides in the bushes, afraid of his own tail. Or perhaps you put on a good act, a façade, pretending to be tough on the outside like the lion did with Dorothy when they met. The price you pay – you show up without authenticity. It takes a ton of work to put on an act. Wouldn't it be easier just to show up as the authentic YOU? Instead of suppressing your feelings, would it not feel better to be fully self-expressed?

Have you been procrastinating on anything? If so, what decision are you putting off? Hesitation and lack of decision rob you of momentum. And when momentum stops, we don't feel like doing anything. When you fail to make decisions and make them on your you're your confidence disappears. Behind every confidence problem is a self-image or self-worth problem. Instead of recognizing how magnificent you are, the good in others and the good in yourself, your focus is on what you are not. Stop it! Move your focus to your strengths, who you are, and what you want. Focus on doing something positive. Give.

So, what can we learn from the lion? It's time to grow up and take your power back. Don't beat yourself up, give yourself empathy. It takes bravery to recognize you may have some disorganized thinking. It takes bravery to come out of hiding and get some help. It takes bravery to be honest with yourself. Don't confuse courage with your inner wisdom. Your higher self, your inner wisdom, is gentling tugging on you trying to pull you into your light. Sometimes it's the blows that wake us up, that provide us the opportunity to learn a lesson.

When Dorothy smacked the lion on the nose because he was bullying Toto, the lion woke up and let go of his façade. Crying is a form of release. The lion was honest and shared his problem with his new friends. His friends recognized his potential, they saw the greatest within him. He stopped thinking only about himself. He started to help his friends. He put scarecrow back together after the monkeys pulled out his straw, and joined the charge to save and rescue Dorothy from the witch in the castle. He displayed bravery.

The good news is you can learn to quiet your Judge and activate your Sage Powers. You have the power to determine your self-worth, to recognize your greatness. You have the power to change your self-image, Help is always available to those who ask for it. Confidence sells. When you are calibrated to your Sage Powers and you know how to quiet your Judge, you are empowered to love yourself, love discovery, love to create possibilities, have love for meaning and purpose and love makes things happen. You become engaged. Trade your primal force of fear for your primal force of love so you can sell well and sell more. As Christopher Robin said to Winnie the Pooh, "You are braver than you believe, stronger than you seem, and smarter than you think."

"If I only had a Heart" – Harden Not Your Heart

"A heart is not judged by how much you love, but by how much you are loved by others." – The Wizard.

Perhaps you've lost your power from a broken heart and you can relate to the Tinman. I know I have felt those heartaches in my career, perhaps you have as well. Examples include losing a manager or colleague that you really enjoy working with; losing the job that you really loved to some outside transition; Not getting the position or the promotion you truly desired; Realizing the company you were loyal to is not loyal to you. Your heart aches because you realize and appreciate how delicious that experience was. Your heart aches because that experience ended and you are yearning for more. The good news is every commencement brings with it a new beginning; another opportunity to create in the infinite game. Just because one joyful experience ended doesn't mean another is not about to begin. We are playing an infinite game.

Have some empathy with yourself. You are human. You experience joy and sadness, gain and loss. Your emotions give you the vibrational translation to keep you moving in the right direction, toward what you love. You have the ability to put any meaning on your experiences. Everything just is. You get to choose the meaning of your life. The meanings can empower you or disempower you. The question to get present to is, "Are you consciously choosing an empowering meaning or do you react with habitual meanings from past experiences?"

Our hearts break when we become attached to people or things outside in the physical world. Most of us developed habits to "*close at the end*" instead of "*opening at the end*" in an effort to protect ourselves from harm. If we close our hearts, we sentence ourselves to a prison of the past and relinquish our power to fear and the illusion of security.

It's the closing that constricts, that cuts you off from your inner power. Closing the heart is turning off the vibrational translator. When you are cut off from the vine, your source of life and spirit, movement ceases. You, like Tinman, rust. You lose your mobility and ability to spread your primal spirit of love.

How do you catch the closing feeling, let go, release, and stay open? Nonresistant thought. Appreciation. Believe in yourself. Serve others. Ask yourself how you can share your love with more people. Make a game of it – how much love can I spread today? The trick is to feel the contrast, let it go, and remember to appreciate what you learned.

With that information, ask yourself what can I create now? What is the gift here? How can you honor the person or relationship you lost? How can you use the gift of the lesson to empower yourself and others? How can you look through this experience from the lens of unconditional love? How can you be content in the uncertainty and have the freedom to create in the new field of possibility? What do you need to notice, appreciate, or believe to spiral yourself upwards toward joy? The electromagnetic force of your heart is what your spirit flows through. Keep your heart open and unleash your spirit of love!

"There's no place like home."

You always have the power to get back home, to return to your inner power and align with source energy. Dorothy told Glenda the good witch what she learned. She said, "*My heart's desire is in my own backyard. If it isn't there, I never lost it to begin with.*"

When you assume your power and claim it you have confidence in your ability to create in the field of possibility; to make lemonade from the lemons; You understand the kingdom of your fulfillment lies within you. You continuously display your ability to transmute and transform whatever is in front of you with ease. When you sell and serve from your heart, you guide others in their transformation. You master the art of listening to your internal guidance system. You use your mental faculties to cause your life and help other people solve problems. You create order where the disorder exists.

Today the world is moving faster than ever before. There are no mistakes in life, just lessons. Life is always happening for you. Life is gently urging you to listen to your heart and assume control of your attention to channel your energy without effort toward what you love, to serve for the harmonious benefit of all concerned. Greatness is within you. Greatness is recognizing your greatest asset and putting it to use.

You have the power. You can give it away or claim it. When you claim it, you say YES to you! You become the cause of your life and live life on your terms. You know you are the cause of your own virtual reality. The more power you access, the more you can give. You become the wizard and you cause the magic! Discover your Courage, follow your heart, channel your focus, and Find Your Way Back Home!

Commencement: The Phoenix and Your Magic Lamp

"If *thou canst believe, all things are possible to him that believeth.*" Mark 9:23

"*Therefore, I say unto you, what things soever ye desire, when ye pray, believe that ye receive them, and ye shall have them.*" Mark 11:24

"*The talent entrusted to you is the power to consciously determine your assumption.*" – Neville Goddard

"*Desire is the effort of an unexpressed possibility within you, attempting to express itself through you in a physical form.*" – Wallace Wattles

"Sow a thought and you reap an action; sow an act and you reap a habit; sow a habit and you reap a character; sow a character and you reap a destiny." Ralph Waldo Emerson

So now that you understand the rules of the game, are you ready to play full out? Let's get into the spirit of the game – the Spirit of Selling! Spirit is movement. It invigorates you, its thriving, it inspires you into action; it enlivens the sales process. When you love what you are doing with great interest, you have tapped into the state of being truly alive; it is that good feeling of which you can never have too much. To enter into the spirit of selling is to make yourself one in thought with the spirit of life itself, universal law, and recognize that life in you!

In the history of the world, there has never been anyone exactly like you and there never will be anyone like you again. You can ordain your destiny by directing your thoughts and controlling your emotions. The physical side of you is here to serve and create. Generating new ideas and implementing them is the most exciting part of selling. It does require work and persistence, but there is nothing more exciting than creating solutions to problems and ways to help your clients that would not have existed without the power of your mind. You matter.

Your mind is your greatest sales asset. Selling is 95% mindset, 5% mechanics. The positive power of life is spirit. The negative power is not spirit. The opposite of spirit is mechanics; both exist. Spirit is the origination source; mechanics are the effect. A mechanical attitude of mind judges everything by the limitations of past experiences, from experiences that likely were a result of ignorance of spiritual law. When we enter into the mechanism of selling, we limit our spirit's freedom. When we enter and operate from the Spirit of Selling, we are at the cause, free to create with infinite supply and abundance.

The Spirit of Selling is being tapped into the state of being truly alive because you understand the wholeness of what you are. You become fearless. You are a center of distribution for transformation and growth. You understand you operate on three planes, your trinity. Source energy, the intellectual plane, and the physical plane. Source energy is the provider, you are a distribution center for source energy with an intellect to create, and in a physical body to serve.

You chose a career in sales for a reason. The greatest honor we have as professional sales people is to serve people powerfully and guide them toward their desired transformation. Every new transformation that we experience individually or by being the guide for our client's transformation, causes momentum and an upward spiral in our evolution.

I want to leave you with a symbol to remind you how simple this process is. Allow me to introduce you to the Phoenix and your Magic lamp. A Phoenix is a mythical bird. Legend states the bird cycles to death and is reborn from its own ashes; The Phoenix is symbolic for renewal and rebirth, transformation through resurrection. The ashes symbolize a purification process; the death of the old and birth of the new. The process is infinite. Your soul, your spirit, is a divine center of operation that works through your marvelous mind. You have the power to create your environment, your habits, and your results either by design or default.

The Phoenix is the real you, your state of awareness, and your concept of yourself that is forever for expansion and fuller expression. You are Spirit. The more awareness you gain of who you really are, and the more you enter into the spirit of the game of selling, you will establish actions and reactions that will vivify you with a continuous momentum of joy. You will always want more; and there will always be change because everything in the universe is moving. The fact that everything is always moving and changing is a blessing. It enables the infinite game for you to create! Your success or failure to meet the challenges of change in the infinite game is dependent upon your use of your invisible powers. Your invisible powers reside in the lamp.

The magic lamp represents a gateway to another plane. Think of the gateway as the bridge between source energy and your distribution center. The gateway bridge provides you what you need to get you from where you are to where you want to go. The source of supply is infinite. The bridge for the supply is built on belief, applied faith. The gateway has a built-in communication system that works like a two-way radio channel communicating by vibration. In all waking moments, you are creating your own point of attraction. Everything is coming to you based upon your vibrational stance. This attraction is magnetic, only things of the same vibration can join you. What you attract depends upon the thoughts you think and the emotions you feel. If you direct the power in the lamp with an intention, and control the vibration, your wishes come true. If you allow outside forces to determine your thoughts or control your feelings, you have no power. Your magic lamp is your marvelous mind. Simply put, all life comes from source through the gateway to the physical plane. The more open and expansive the gateway becomes; the more spirit can flow and expand.

So, what if anything, blocks up the gateway? Why do you to bump into walls and hit glass ceilings? There is only one insidious villain you face that robs you of the abundance of sales you desire and the control of your power.

This villain causes sales mayhem with your:

- Perception/Attitude

- Use of Time

- Creativity

- Effectiveness

- Productivity

- Logic

- Ability to earn Money

It hides in all of your agreements, and if you are not aware of it, watching for it, and ready to dispel it, it will rob you of your dreams and your success. If you do not address the villain, you've gone as far as you will go.

Your villain is your own **self-imposed disbelief**. Disbelief is the *inability* or *refusal* to accept that something is true or real. Disbelief is thinking you cannot have what you want. Disbelief is negative in polarity. Disbelief is Judgement. Disbelief is the opposite of Belief. Disbelief contradicts. Disbelief is unbelief and your infinite source of supply does not exist in unbelief.

How often have you heard someone say, "It's too good to be true?" That comment sounds harmless, yet it is a show stopper. **You have two invisible powers of attraction that are true and good**. They are belief and a positive attitude. Combined they create a source of powerful magnetism. They are your attraction managers. These powers are activated by *congruency*; Congruency of thought and belief and congruency of thought with action. It's the mixture that determines the power or lack of power. If you try to make bread without the yeast, the bread will not rise. If your super power components are congruent, in harmony, the power activates. If any component is contradictory, the superpower is rendered powerless.

Very few people take the time to sit down and evaluate their beliefs. Most of us get in a habit of defending them! What would your life be like if you used a computer programmed in 1990 to run your life in 2021? A computer that had no updates in thirty years? You would not tolerate that, would you? Look how often you are updating your phone! Don't you think your greatest asset needs updating to match your continual desire for more? Are you defending your beliefs to allow you to be pure? To be right? To support your story? Are they really serving you or anyone else?

It's not common practice for people to do introspection on their beliefs. Most people fail to recognize the distinction between their spiritual essence and their beliefs. Beliefs are not you. Beliefs are agreements and conclusions we make. They are ideas we accept as true without question. All the beliefs you have today are from the past. Beliefs are self-perpetuating. And therein lies the paradox and the reason people get stuck. What is true? You can't escape a prison you do not know you are in.

Beliefs are running your programming. Your beliefs control your habits. Ninety-six percent of all human behavior is habitual. Beliefs are not right or wrong but they can cause you self-sabotage. Have you ever said to yourself, "I don't know why I did that?"

Beliefs are agreements you made based upon an evaluation of something you saw, heard, or experienced. You accepted these ideas at the time to be true without evidence. You have financial agreements, spiritual agreements, agreements about money, agreements about sales, relationship agreements, social agreements, and personal agreements. These beliefs are either productive or non-productive; supportive or non-supportive.

We accepted many ideas in our childhood from our Domestication & Attachments. We created a judge, an inner critic to protect us. The inner critic is a source of disbelief. It was created to help us cope with dysfunction, or anything we could not understand at the time. It is the voice that says, "I am not enough," or "I am powerless." This inner critic we created to help us become self-domesticated to keep out of trouble. You can detect disbelief from the Judge by looking for "IF, THEN" statements in your agreements. The IF, THEN in an agreement represents "conditional" love. It shows up when you judge yourself, others, or circumstances. Source energy is unconditional. Your source of supply does not exist except in unconditional love. Any belief that generates fear or feelings of unworthiness is false; it's a lie. If you have no belief in yourself and what you are capable of, you miss out on revealing and experiencing your divinity.

Remember you have divinity within. You are perfect. Your beliefs were developed from spaced based repetition and they became habitual. Habitual for so long, that you forgot about them. Beliefs shape your conditioning and act like a cybernetic instrument to keep you in line with your programming, on auto-pilot. With an open mind, focused on opening the gateway, you have the power to re-evaluate and reframe your beliefs using your attitude and perception powers. You can allow yourself to choose new beliefs based on who you are today and who you want to become. Accept only those that are productive and supportive for you NOW. Build a new belief that matches your current desire and values.

Belief is one of your two invisible powers; it is what causes transformation. Belief is applied faith without evidence. Faith is guidance. Applied faith is taking that guidance and putting it into action. Remember you are the instrument, the distribution center from which the source energy flows. You comply with the laws.

Beliefs are present in the conscious and subconscious mind. Congruency is the activator. A new belief in the conscious mind is male energy and requires belief in the subconscious mind of female energy to fuse with it to give rise to its birth.

That means you must put some emotion behind it. Get out of you head and into your heart, feel it. Act in a state of expectancy just like a child who believes in Santa Claus does. I believed in Santa up until I was twelve. The process was to sit on Santa's lap, tell him what you wanted and believe. I would then start imagining what it was going to be like to have my new bike or toy and play with it in my dreams. I was totally into the spirit of receiving! The tradition is a great way to instill the power of belief that works by controlled attention of the will with imagination.

You can only attract to you, your vibrational match. Ask yourself, "What does it feel like now that it is done?" Use your imagination. They say imagination is the only redemptive power of the universe where transformation can take place. Imagination is the workshop where we can shape energy and ideas into concepts for manifestations. Just like cement hardens when it comes in contact with water, Ideas harden into fact when ideas come in contact with a positive assumption or belief.

Remember disbelief is the villain that repels desire. Allow yourself to release the old belief and activate the new one! Think about how many people besides you will benefit from you adopting the new belief. How many more people will be served? Unless all disbelief is purified and removed, no matter how hard the conscious mind tries, no manifestation from the power will occur without the emotion of belief. Activate your super power with congruency.

Attitude is typically mirrored unless mastered. This magic power allows you to transmute, to change form. Attitude is your perception faculty. The components of attitude must be congruent for mastery. Attitude is the composite of your thoughts, feelings, and actions. It is your perception, how you view your world. Attitude is an energy field. Whatever you put out comes back to you by attraction. Attitude is how you show up when circumstances are pleasant and how you show up under stress and unpleasant circumstances. It's what you bring to the party. Congruency gives you the ability to hold your attitude steady regardless of the attitude of those around you. If the three components, your thoughts, feelings, and actions are not aligned, no super power activates. You will revert to the habitual pattern of mirroring what is around you and be at the effect of outside circumstances. If your thoughts, feelings, and actions are congruent, aimed in a positive manner like nature, you have the power to move mountains. Why? Because you are aligned in perfect harmony with universal source and universal law.

Okay, it all sounds easy, but why do many people struggle to make sales happen? Because they have not built up their mental muscle strength for congruency. Say you want to earn three hundred thousand dollars in commission this year. The most you ever earned was two hundred thousand. You sit down and calculate the math to know the quantity of customers, products, and services needed to generate that commission. You have conscious belief from the logic. But there is no inspiration in the logic. And your inner critic, the judge in your subconscious mind says "Who do you think you are? You've never done more than two hundred thousand." And others around you tell you, "That's impossible." Are you going to buy into that or are you going to affirm the "I am possible attitude?"

If you do not know how to shut down that judge program and shift to your sage powers, you will not have the emotional feeling of confidence and it will not happen. You have not gotten yourself emotionally involved with something bigger than you, an aim that it not just about you. The easiest way to create a feeling of expectancy and belief is to jump into action and think about what you CAN DO instead of what you cannot do. Henry Ford used his will power to do that when he refused to accept that a V-8 engine was not possible. When you direct your thoughts and action toward what you can do, all of a sudden momentum builds and you bring your emotions in line to a solid state of confidence, courage, and competency. You have mastered your transformation power by congruency.

Here's an attitude example. Say you are in a medical device startup company. FDA approval of the device is delayed.

Cash flow is being depleted and everyone around you is caught up in fear. Will you engage in the gossip of worry and doubt? Or will your thoughts, feelings, and action stay fixed firmly on what you can do to create value and contribute to solve a problem? Will you look for the good and find it? Will you focus on what you can do? Will you stand in a congruent state, creating magic knowing that no matter what happens, something good is present and will unfold? Remember every adversity has the seed of an equivalent or greater benefit. A negative mental attitude contains disbelief, your insidious villain. Contradiction in any form will result in failure and struggle. Congruency, staying focused on what you want, what you can do, and looking for the good will result in effortless success. Do not get attached to an outcome become attached to giving and serving; staying at the cause. You have the power to direct your thoughts, control your emotions, and regulate your attitude. Master your ability to transmute. Remember the boomerang law, you get back what you put out.

Now you know the villain and your invisible powers. So, are you ready to take your transformation and transmutation power back? Never to surrender it again? All it takes in an alignment process. Follow these three steps:

1) **Allow yourself to evaluate your agreements**. Remind yourself that abundance requires belief to keep the supply coming to your distribution center. Rid yourself of the "GET" mindset. It is based on lack and scarcity. Eliminate worry and doubt. Affirm you are more than enough and that you are powerful. All you have to do is activate your super powers with belief.

2) Make a **committed decision** to be at the cause of your results versus the effect. You know the type I am talking about. It's when you pull the rip cord and say "That's it – no more!" If you think back on every major decision you made in your life, you will remember how everything shifted at that moment. Why? You changed your vibrational frequency. At that point you refused to be controlled by the old habit. You tapped into

the will power, like that of John Wick or Napoleon. You set your sail and burned your bridges. Utilize Ben Franklin's virtues when you make your decisions. For example, do not make decisions based on fear; you cannot hear your intuition in a state of fear. Reason and memory only work well when you have temperance in the body. Ensure you are in a positive mental attitude, looking for the good and how you can calibrate to your joy. Exercise your will power with determination. If you take your power back you can and will cause permanent change. The only requirement is desire. You do not have to know the how.

3) **Choose a new productive habit** and refuse to believe it is not true. Purify and remove the old non-productive habit. Practice your habit with persistence for thirty days and then cosmic habit force will kick in and you will keep soaring to new heights.

Need help? I offer these services to get started.

1) **Energy Leadership Index Assessment** – This assessment provides a unique lens on your self-awareness

and emotional intelligence, it illustrates how you show up, two key ingredients for any leader. Situational awareness of yourself and others is critical for a leader to respond appropriately to the people in their charge. Understanding where you are at any moment and how you respond to stress can make all the difference.

2) **Mental muscle workouts** - I offer my coaching clients an active app they can use daily for 15 minutes to strengthen mental muscle to favor habitual positive behavior. This is a value-add service that comes with my coaching and mentorship. Learn more here - https://www.positiveintelligence.com/pq-score/

3) **Coaching and sales training services** – Step into your courage, confidence, and competence to improve your sales, perception, use of time, effectiveness, productivity, creativity, and ability to earn money. Team virtual or live sales training services focused on behavioral change based on the principles behind the Spirit of Selling. Lead the field in your industry by the application of principles

based in emotional intelligence, attitude and belief to sell well and sell more.

For more information on my products and services go to https://www.3x5coaching.com

By now, with study, you understand universal law gives order and thought is movement. You are the instrument, the co-creator, who channels source energy for the harmonious good of all concerned. Your thoughts are powerful and have the ability to shape and transform energy. Your mental faculties are your greatest powers and when you begin to use them purposefully to sell and serve, working with the principles of universal law, you cannot lose. By calibrating yourself to source energy, which is where your joy resides, you can't help but leave everyone with an impression of increase. You are a change agent capable of guiding people through their transformations to experience more peace, joy, and fulfilment. The greatest gifts you can bestow on yourself and others is the gift of your belief and your positive mental attitude.

Your product or service solves a problem for your client that could be personal, professional, or philosophical. Transformation of conditions and character are a natural part of our evolution and entropy as human beings. There are opportunities everywhere and today there are over 7.6 billion people evolving on the planet and looking for guides like you. Very few have understood the principles of transformation, but now you do and you can be their *best* guide. With this wisdom and understanding all the old limitations will pass away and you can now live at the center of an entirely new world of life, liberty and love. This is your distribution center. Knowledge of the principles behind transformation allows you to navigate, explore, innovate, and activate creation with empathy while selling.

Every human being has greatness within. You have the power, the assets, that can reveal and bring forth the desires and infinite possibilities for your clients into physical manifestations You have the potential to continually transform yourself, your character, and your awareness to soar to infinite new heights.

When you take control of your mind you become the captain of your soul. You sell well because you:

-control and adjust your perception;

- control your attention with your willpower;

- listen to your intuition;

- create in your imagination;

-utilize your past and future memory ability;

- display the ability to utilize inductive reasoning with your critical thinking skills.

Truth is energy, and emotion is your power source, the reality of you.

Spirit is invisible but magical.

Spirit is life;

Spirit is expansion and greater expression.

Spirit is love;

Spirit is light;

Spirit is power;

Spirit is peace;

Spirit is beauty;

Spirit is joy and bliss

You get to write the conclusion from this book. This commencement is your new beginning and today is the first day of the rest of your life. Get into action, share your spirit – its where the receiving happens!

Remember: *You are the cause. The sale is the effect.*

Grow, Give, Serve and Transform.

Sell by Law, not by Luck. Get into the spirit of the Game –
Get into the Spirit of Selling!

More Tips and Tools to keep you in the Spirit of Selling can be

found at https://www.thespiritofselling.com

About the Author

Rhonda Petit is a Sales and Business Peak Performance Coach with over 35 years of Sales and Sales Management experience in Corporate America in the life sciences and diagnostic markets. She has experience working with Fortune 500 and Fortune 1000 companies. Today she works enthusiastically with Corporations and Individuals with champion mindsets, who know school is never out, who want to continually grow to unleash and activate more of their true potential and power. She helps people discover their deepest desires, leverage the untapped potential in their hearts, activate their potential and achieve their personal and professional goals so they can create the life they want and realize true fulfillment.

Rhonda is a seasoned Sales Professional, a certified coach, leader, in-demand speaker, and author of "The Spirit of Selling." She loves Sales and Coaching. Everyone is in sales whether they realize it or not.

Rhonda offers services for personal and professional development as well as sales skills and leadership training. She is excited about changing the culture of Corporate America to one that recognizes their employees as

The Spirit of Selling

their most precious asset and their professional development their strongest competitive advantage.

By working with Rhonda corporations and individuals benefit from an environment at work and home that embodies critical thinking, imagination, cooperation, collaboration, creativity, connection, and fun!

Clients that work with Rhonda experience quantum leaps in their performance and a sense of true fulfillment in their work.

 www.3x5coaching.com

Email: info@3x5coaching.com

Made in the USA
Middletown, DE
11 October 2021

50078632R00205